D0629085

NO MORE STRESS!

NO MORE STRESS!

Be Your Own Stress Management Coach

Gladeana McMahon

KARNAC

First published in 2011 by
Karnac Ltd.
118 Finchley Road, London NW3 5HT

Copyright © 2011 Gladeana McMahon.

The right of Gladeana McMahon to be identified as the
author of this work has been asserted in accordance with
§§ 77 and 78 of the Copyright Design and Patents Act 1988.

All rights reserved. No part of this publication may be
reproduced, stored in a retrieval system, or transmitted,
in any form or by any means, electronic, mechanical,
photocopying, recording, or otherwise, without the prior
written permission of the publisher.

British Library Cataloguing in Publication Data

A C.I.P. for this book is available from the British Library

   ISBN: 978 1 88575 501 7

Edited, designed, and produced by
The Studio Publishing Services Ltd
www.publishingservicesuk.co.uk
e-mail: studio@publishingservicesuk.co.uk

www.karnacbooks.com

ACC LIBRARY SERVICES AUSTIN, TX

Contents

Contents

Contents

To all my clients who have allowed me
to share their challenges

About the author

Gladeana McMahon is considered one of the leading personal development and transformational coaches in the UK. She combines academic rigour with down to earth communication skills. She holds a range of qualifications and is accredited with the British Association for Counselling and Psychotherapy, Association of Rational Emotive Behaviour Practitioners, and the British Association for Behavioural and Cognitive Psychotherapies as both a therapist and a coach.

She helped to found the Association for Coaching, in which she holds the positions of Fellow and Vice President. Gladeana is also a Fellow of the British Association for Counselling and Psychotherapy, Institute of Management Studies, and Royal Society of Arts. As an innovator, she is one of the UK founders of Cognitive Behavioural Coaching and an internationally published author with some twenty books of a popular and academic nature on coaching and counselling to her name. She has presented a range of coaching programmes, and was listed as one of the UK's Top Ten Coaches by both the *Independent on Sunday* and *Observer on Sunday*, and as one of the UK's Top Twenty Therapists by the *Evening Standard*.

Gladeana is the kind of woman who will have you saying, '*Don't say I can't – say how can I and believing it*!' (*Independent on Sunday*).

INTRODUCTION

What's special about a cognitive–behavioural approach?

The problem with using words like counselling, psycho-therapy, or coaching is that these words suggest there is only one model or method of practice. However, at the last count there were some 450 different therapeutic approaches and there are now many models of coaching, some sharing ideas in common and others being as different as chalk and cheese.

Cognitive–Behaviour Therapy is a relatively new therapy. Behaviour Therapy came first in the mid-1950s, aimed originally at helping people deal with the symptoms of depression by changing the things that they did. Although Behaviour Therapy was a movement forward as it provided many people with real benefits, it also became apparent that something was lacking, and this turned out to be attention to individual thoughts that accompanied behaviour.

In the late 1960s, Cognitive Therapy came into being and this therapy focused on the types of thinking styles that caused people distress. It was not long before the benefits of Behaviour and Cognitive Therapy came together, forming what is now called Cognitive–Behaviour Therapy, often referred to as CBT. Cognitive–Behaviour Therapy is the only therapy that has sought to put itself forward for assessment and validation through research, its practitioners believing it important that a therapy should not only work but should demonstrate how it works and

1

why. As with all therapies, it has developed over the years from a way of helping people with depression to a therapy that can help individuals with a number of mental health conditions. There are now many studies supporting the view that the treatment of choice for a range of conditions is CBT, and, indeed, the National Institute for Clinical Excellence (NICE) and the National Health Service (NHS) have both recommended CBT as the premier treatment when working with conditions such as depression, anxiety, anger, and stress.

In 2002, Professors Windy Dryden and Stephen Palmer, together with Michael Neenan and myself, went on to consider ways in which Cognitive–Behaviour Therapy could be adapted into a coaching model, which we named Cognitive Behavioural Coaching (CBC). By adapting many of the strategies associated with CBT, we were able to put together a model that helped individuals get the best from everyday life. In addition, by integrating aspects from the new field of Positive Psychology, which aims to increase an individual's basic appreciation of life and general happiness, I was able to produce a model that worked for everyone and not just those with an identifiable mental health problem.

HOW WILL THIS BOOK HELP ME?

This book takes the skills and techniques of Cognitive–Behavioural Therapy and Cognitive–Behavioural Coaching to offer you the opportunity of taking control of your stress. The book aims to help you understand what is happening to you and teaches you how to overcome stress. If you use and practise the skills in this book, you will learn how to become your own stress management coach.

Some of you may find it helpful to read the book through once before returning to do the exercises. Others may find it more helpful to tackle each of the exercises as they come up. It is up to you to decide which method suits you best. What is important is that you work through the book at your own pace and in your own time, making sure that you understand each and every exercise. Don't skip an exercise just because you think you do not need it; you might not, but many people have thought that and then gone on to find that they benefited from the exercise in question. Change will only come about if you practise the skills in your everyday life. Don't expect your behaviour to change overnight, as it took you time to be the person you are and it will take time to change yourself. Be realistic and praise yourself for every change you make, however small you think it is. Remember that you are doing something positive to coach yourself, and even if you find it difficult, you have taken the first step to help yourself.

For some people, using the skills in this book may be enough to become stress free. For others, the book will help to reduce the stress you experience. For some readers, this book may make little difference at all. If you are in this last category, do not see this as a failure on your part, but rather as an indication that you require specialist help. Your doctor can refer you for Cognitive–Behaviour Therapy, or you can visit www.babcp.com and find a list of Cognitive–Behavioural Therapists you can see privately. You may benefit from Cognitive Behavioural Coaching for Stress, and the Association for Coaching UK has a list of coaches you can select at www.associationforcoaching.com. Alternatively, if you contact ISMA (International Stress Management Association) (www.isma.org.uk), you can find a list of stress management coaches who may also be able to assist you.

The fact that you are reading this book means that you want to do something about the stress you experience, and if you have that kind of motivation, then specialist stress management counselling or coaching is likely to be of great benefit to you.

What materials will I need?

You will need to get yourself a journal or an A4 loose-leaf folder that you can use to track your progress and in which you should do the exercises. Do not write your answers to the exercises in the book itself, since you will not be able to see how things change as you progress. Change does not happen overnight (it is worth saying again), and there will be times when you may feel that you are not making as much progress as you thought or would like to. However, by keeping all your work in one place, you will be able to see that even if you are having a bad day, changes are happening, maybe just not as quickly as you would want. Remember that bad days get shorter and good days get longer, but there are likely to be setbacks as this is normal. Your journal is a good way of capturing the total picture, and helps you to maintain a realistic appraisal of what you have managed to achieve. In addition, research has shown that if you write things down, you are more likely to achieve the goals you set for yourself.

WHAT IS STRESS?

Too much of a good thing – the stress response

Biologically, our bodies produce a range of stress hormones, such as adrenalin, that encourage changes in your physical and mental state, helping you either to escape from the situation or face it head-on. This is called the 'stress response', and you may have heard it called 'fight or flight'. The three key players that come into play when it comes to the stress hormones are adrenalin (associated with flight), noradrenalin (associated with fight), and cortisol (a kind of on/off switch).

When you experience this type of reaction, you often feel muscle tension and an increase in heart rate, breathing, and blood pressure. You may sweat, and experience changes in your digestive system such as 'butterflies' in the stomach. Your thinking can become more focused on the task ahead, and you may be able to do things that you would not normally be able to. You may have heard stories of people who have undertaken superhuman feats to save a loved one. For example, a colleague is trapped in a fire under a cabinet that has fallen on him and a friend is able to lift cabinet to free him – something that under normal circumstances would seem impossible as it would be far too heavy to lift.

There is a third response that can be triggered and this is the 'freeze' response, where the person stops and becomes very still and is unable to move. Although this is a less common response, it can be very effective in the right circumstances – for example, if you were hiding from an attacker.

The stress response is a survival strategy, and is your body's way of providing you with a biological mechanism to deal with life-threatening situations. When you step into the road and suddenly see a car speeding towards you that is unlikely to stop, you want to be able to move as quickly as possible to get out of the way. It is just this type of situation that the stress response is designed to help you with. However, many people become severely stressed over situations that are far from life threatening, and it is when this happens that problems occur.

Like anything in life, too much of a good thing can become a problem. The stress response is essential, and yet, for many, it has become a burden rather than a blessing.

Figure 1 shows you what happens to your body when it experiences the stress response.

The stress response is your body's natural defence system for dealing with danger. If activated for short periods, the stress response will not cause you undue harm. If activated and sustained over long periods of time, you are likely to experience both psychological and physical damage.

The stress response can also have an impact on personal performance. Figure 2 shows how your ability to cope is affected by stress when it is experienced over longer periods of time. At first, your performance may well improve, but as time goes on, you become exhausted and your performance decreases.

The physical, mental, and behavioural sensations associated with 'fight or flight' that are essential for managing those life-threatening crisis situations, however, can turn into something quite different when the stress response is not turned off.

7

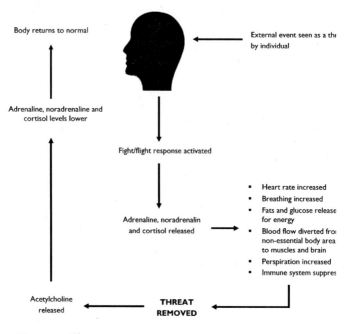

Body returns to normal

External event seen as a thr
by individual

Adrenaline, noradrenaline and
cortisol levels lower

Fight/flight response activated

Adrenaline, noradrenalin
and cortisol released

- Heart rate increased
- Breathing increased
- Fats and glucose release
  for energy
- Blood flow diverted fro
  non-essential body area
  to muscles and brain
- Perspiration increased
- Immune system suppres

Acetylcholine
released

**THREAT
REMOVED**

Figure 1.   The stress response

PERFORMANCE

COPING ABILITY

BEST PERFORMANCE

EFFECTIVE

LESS EFFICIENT

LESS CREATIVE

CREATIVE

DECISIVE

POOR CONCENTRATION

ALERT

INDECISIVE

IRRITABLE

ANXIOUS

BOREDOM

FRUSTRATION

EXHAUSTION

PRESSURES

Figure 2.   Personal performance levels

8

A list of stress related symptoms is given in Table 1.

Table 1.   Stress-related symptoms

Physical	Emotional signs
Tightness in chest	Mood swings
Chest pain and/or palpitations	Feeling anxious/worrying more
Indigestion	Feeling tense
Breathlessness	Feeling angry
Nausea	Feeling guilty
Muscle twitches	Feelings of shame
Aches and pains	Having no enthusiasm
Headaches	Becoming more cynical
Skin conditions	Feeling out of control
Recurrence of previous illnesses/allergies	Feeling helpless
Constipation/diarrhoea	Decrease in confidence/ self-esteem
Weight loss or weight gain	Poor concentration
Change in menstrual cycle for women	
Fainting	
Tiredness	

Behaviour	Thoughts/psychological aspects
Drop in work performance	"I am a failure"
More inclined to become accident-prone	'I should be able to cope'
Drinking and smoking more	'Why is everyone getting at me?'
Overeating/loss of appetite	'No one understands'
Change in sleeping patterns	'I don't know what to do'
Poor time management	'I can't cope'
Too busy to relax	Loss of judgement
Stuttering	Withdrawing from family and friends
Loss of interest in sex	Poor judgement
Inability to express feelings	A sense of being on a kind of 'automatic pilot'
Emotional outbursts and over-reactions	
Nervous habits such as drumming fingers	

So, what exactly happens to my body when I become stressed?

Stress is experienced in your body as well as in your mind, and there is a complex series of physiological changes that occurs as you become stressed.

Emotions begin inside two almond-shaped structures in your brain that are called the amygdala. The amygdala is the part of the brain responsible for identifying threats to our well-being, and for sending out an alarm when threats are identified so that you can take steps to protect yourself. The amygdala is so good at sending you warning signals about possible threats that you may often react before the part of the brain responsible for thought and judgement (the cortex) is able to check on whether your actions are reasonable or not. This could be seen as a case of 'act first and think later', which means that you do not have time to consider the consequences of your behaviour.

As you become stressed, your body's muscles tense up. Inside your brain, neurotransmitter chemicals known as catecholamines are released so that you experience a spurt of energy lasting up to several minutes, and your body releases a series of stress hormones, as mentioned above. This energy is behind the desire to take immediate protective action. Your heart rate accelerates, your blood pressure rises, and your rate of breathing increases. Your blood flow increases as you prepare for physical action, and your body releases fatty acids to give you more energy. Additional brain neurotransmitters and hormones (such as adrenalin and noradrenalin) are released, which trigger a state of arousal and you are now ready either to stay in the situation and defend yourself (fight), or else to get away as quickly as possible (flight).

Some statistics about stress

In 2007, the Health and Safety Commission estimated that workplace stress cost the UK £530 million in the problems associated with individuals suffering from the condition. The 2009 Psychosocial Working Conditions (PWC) survey indicated that around 16.7% of all working individuals thought their job was very, or extremely, stressful. Between 2006 and 2008, surveillance data from general practitioners indicated that 30.9% of all diagnoses of work-related ill-health are cases of mental ill-health. Sleep problems, depression, and anxiety are the most commonly experienced problems associated with stress. Weight management issues also come into play, as cortisol has been linked with an increase in appetite, which is why when you become stressed you may turn towards high calorie foods such as fats and sugar as it is your body's way of trying to get as much energy as possible, as quickly as possible, into your system to keep you ready for action. If you were running a marathon, this would be a good idea. However, as most people are just going about their daily lives and not using up the energy from these foods, this usually means putting on weight. In addition, if you are already predisposed to conditions such as eczema or psoriasis, you may find that these get worse or re-occur, even if you have not experienced them since childhood.

So, just how stressed am I?

Although you are already aware that you have some difficulty with stress (otherwise you would not be reading this book), Table 2 provides you with a check-list of the signs

Gladeana McMahon

Table 2.   Signs that you have difficulties with your stress

Signs	Tick boxes
I don't seem able to stop worrying these days	☐
I feel drained	☐
I find it hard to sleep	☐
I seem to be more irritable these days	☐
I seem to have more headaches and feelings of tension	☐
I am not really interested in people these days	☐
I find it hard to focus on the task in hand	☐

Thoughts

What's the point when everything seems too much?	☐
I'll do it later, can't be bothered now	☐
I just can't get through everything	☐
I wish people would stop asking things of me	☐
It's just one thing after another	☐

Feelings

Irritability	☐
Sadness	☐
Feeling tense and uptight	☐

Psychological factors

Loss of concentration	☐
My life seems like one big problem	☐
I can't think straight	☐

Bodily sensations

Tight chest	☐
Pounding heart	☐
Churned-up stomach	☐
Tense muscles	☐
Feeling hot	☐
Legs feel weak	☐
Craving sugar and foods I don't normally eat	☐
Aches and pains	☐
Getting more minor colds and flu bugs than normal	☐
Feeling more tired than usual	☐

and symptoms that outline just how much difficulty you really have. The more ticks you have, the more difficulty you are likely to experience.

Place a tick against any of the following statements that you believe apply to you.

Are some people more susceptible?

There is still much research required to assess whether some people are truly genetically predisposed to stress and, if so, by how much. There is some evidence to suggest that this may be the case, since, for example, research demonstrates that mothers who experience extreme stress while pregnant pass on an excess of stress hormones to their unborn child, which, in turn, makes the child less tolerant to withstanding stress. Therefore, it does seem reasonable to make the assumption that there may well be additional genetic components that have not yet come to light.

However, there are a number of factors associated with the unhelpful experience of stress. These are family history, stressful life events, thinking style, poor coping skills, individual personality, and lack of social support. Even if the geneticists go on to discover other biological factors that predispose an individual towards stress, it is important to understand that a predisposition does not have to be a life sentence. For example, an individual could be predisposed towards a condition such as heart problems. However, if that person eats well, exercises, and leads a healthy lifestyle, they may never go on to develop the disease. Therefore, it is important to recognize that even if some people are more predisposed towards stress, this does not necessarily mean that they will automatically be a victim of their predisposition.

It is interesting to note that Sonya Lyubomirsky and colleagues at the University of California conducted a study in which they looked at all the available research on genetic predisposition. They concluded that, in the worst possible case, it was likely that only fifty per cent of diffi-culties would emanate from genetic predisposition, while ten per cent of difficulties could be put down to life events. Even if you take this sixty per cent as a true figure, it would mean that there is forty per cent within the indi-vidual's control. I stress that the fifty per cent would be the worst possible case scenario. Looking at it this way, most people are not going to fall into the worst case scenario and, therefore, you are more likely to have sixty, seventy, or even eighty per cent going for you, and that the genetic component is much smaller than anyone would think. I do not know about you, but if I were a betting person I would be very happy with these odds, as they would suggest that far more is within my control than not.

Family history

Research tends to show that stress and the inability to deal with stress often runs in families. As yet, no one really knows how much this is due to genetic influences and how much is down to learning unhelpful behaviours and self-defeating thinking styles from family members. Even if you are born into a family whose members are predisposed to stress, it does not automatically mean that you are doomed for life to become a stressed person. Much of our behaviour is learnt, and, if a behaviour or way of thinking can be learnt, it can be unlearnt, and new behaviours developed if the individual is prepared to put some work in.

Stressful life events

Everyone experiences stressful periods from time to time. Sometimes these events take the form of bereavement, job loss, or relationship problems. Any event where we feel threatened is likely to induce some kind of stressful feelings. Psychologists discovered that even pleasant experiences, such as having a child or gaining a promotion, could be stressful, as they also contain change; too much change, even positive change, requires a degree of emotional readjustment.

Thinking style

People who think in certain ways are more likely to feel stressed. Such thinking styles include the ability to discount the positive (always putting down or dismissing anything positive that is said) or maximizing negative events by being overly pessimistic and dramatic. In particular, beliefs about justice and fairness, and whether we see people as basically benevolent or out to get us, are likely to trigger stressful feelings. There will be more about this type of negative thinking and the relevant antidotes later in this book. Research has shown that there is a strong link between what you think and the mood you feel. The more negative your thinking, the more stressed you are likely to feel, particularly when the thoughts are based on perceptions of threat or on injustice.

For example, Jane worked hard and was doing well in her job. She put in more hours than her colleagues, and had recently been promoted. Everyone viewed her as being very fair and approachable. Her new manager was someone with a reputation for being difficult, and it seemed to Jane that she could never do anything right to please her new manager, however hard she tried. She found herself putting in even more hours and never getting any recognition or praise. After a year, Jane found that she was exhausted, and experienced intense feelings of stress, based on her sense that what was happening was just not fair. Many people may feel that Jane had a point; she was working hard and doing a good job. However, had Jane stood back and assessed the situation and not expected her manager to be the same as her, she would have realized that her manager had a completely different personality and that the best way to deal with the situation was to depersonalize it, not keep on trying to gain her manager's approval, but continue to do a good job and become more assertive in her communications and more realistic in her attitudes.

Poor coping skills

Many of you will have some excellent coping skills that you can call on when you need them. For example, you may have learnt that dealing with things that need to be done, rather than just thinking about them, decreases your feelings of stress as it gives you a sense of control over the situation. However, most people have some coping strategies that are unhelpful, such as drinking, smoking, or eating too much as a way of comforting themselves.

Individual personality

Your essential personality type is likely either to help or hinder you when it comes to dealing with stress. In the late 1960s, cardiologists discovered what have become to be known as Type A and Type B personalities and, more recently, a third group has been added, called the Hardy Personality. Type As are ambitious, competitive, hard driving, and more likely to ignore stress symptoms. Although Type As have a tremendous capacity when it comes to energy and drive and are often seen as highly productive by those around them, they tend to go down rather spectacularly when they become overloaded. Type Bs are more laid-back and find it easier to keep matters in perspective, whereas the Hardy Personality type seems to have all the attributes of a Type A, but without the susceptibility to stress.

One of the classic symptoms of a stressed Type A is irritability and anger, and even the most charismatic and normally stable Type A character can be prone to angry outbursts over the smallest of issues when they are stressed. Having said that, this does not mean that the Type B or Hardy Personality characters do not get irritable and angry – they do. However, they are less likely to be so, and more likely to take action earlier to deal with whatever is getting on top of them.

Another personality factor is whether you believe that your actions can make a difference. Are you the kind of person who sees yourself as having a choice and some control over what you do, or do you see yourself as always having to deal with forces outside your control?

This type of approach to life is known as your 'locus of control', studies on which date back to the 1960s. The term 'locus of control' describes the degree to which you believe that outcomes result from your own behaviours, or from forces that are external. People who develop an internal locus of control believe that they are responsible for their own success. Those with an external locus of control believe that external forces, such as luck, determine their outcomes. Typically, in life, either extreme end of the spectrum will cause problems. If an individual believes that everything is within his or her control, then, when faced with a situation that no one could control or influence, s/he may find it difficult to accept the reality, experiencing extreme distress as any attempts to change a situation fail. However, if you believe that everything is outside of your control, then you may not take actions to help yourself when you could, and simply attribute events to 'fate'. When we are stressed, as with anything else in life, it is important to appreciate and recognize what we can and what we cannot control. It is helpful to take action that will be useful. However, sometimes there is nothing that can be done and, on these occasions, it is important to ride out the storm.

Social support

Over the years, research has demonstrated that people with good support systems in the form of family and friends are far more likely to ward off the effects of stressful situations. The more people we have to talk to, the more we are protected from the full effect of dealing with stress on our own. A lack of a social network really shows itself in times of crisis. Very often, simply letting off a little steam to a friend or loved one early on can prevent the build-up of pent-up emotion that can later lead to an increase in stress-related symptoms.

Other forms of support

Notwithstanding the importance of social support, during times of crisis, or when we are experiencing stress, it is not uncommon for individuals to find it difficult to think clearly. Even when help is available, an individual may be too busy trying to cope on a daily basis and not always seek help early enough. There are a number of categories that help could fall into.

Physical help: for example, financial advice, physical help such as a home helper or carer, and/or the provision of useful resources.

Political help: for example, finding those individuals with influence who can use this on your behalf.

Information: For example, others may have personal experience that can help you, either because they have experienced the same problem or have helped people who have.

Could I have learnt to be stressed?

It is certainly possible that you could have learnt to be stressed. If one of your parents found life hard to cope with and tended towards getting stressed over the smallest of incidents, you would learn that stress is a natural response. After all, as a child, your parents are the people you look up to and learn from. In certain situations, you would have learnt that life is hard to handle.

It might be helpful to think of childhood as a type of training course where those who look after you are the trainers. If the trainers are well trained and able to pass on the life skills needed, you will go on to develop these skills. However, if, through no fault of the trainers, they do not have the skills, or are going through a bad time that stops them from being able to pass on the skills, then it is likely you will not develop the skills you need.

Is all stress bad?

There is a big difference between 'pressure' and 'stress'. Pressure is healthy and provides the opportunity for individuals to work hard, stretching their abilities, and many people thrive on it. Stress is only ever experienced when the body's stress response kicks in, depleting your ability to perform effectively. One of the key differences between pressure and stress is whether you feel a sense of personal control over your day-to-day activities.

When someone becomes stressed, the body does not rid itself of the effects of producing too many stress hormones. It is one thing to experience a one-off event or short-term difficulties, and it is another if you are constantly being stretched beyond your physical, emotional, psychological, and behavioural capabilities. In such circumstances, your body never manages to clear the debilitating side effects of the stress hormones and it is this build-up of these that undermines your physical state and performance.

For example, when produced consistently, adrenalin associated with both excitement and fear can cause problems with the body's adrenal system, as it is associated with tiredness and sleeplessness. Excessive production of cortisol can destroy brain cells, leading to short-term memory problems.

It has been argued that producing stress hormones on a short-term basis can make an individual more effective, given the boost in energy. This is certainly true; many people talk about an 'adrenalin buzz' when they have had to deal with a pretty challenging period and have said they actually enjoyed the experience. In this sense, the individual is rising to the short-term need to deliver more, and the pleasant effects and sense of alertness that adrenalin can bring are experienced as pleasurable. However, the key is in the word 'short-term'. Many people love theme parks and enjoy what are called 'white knuckle rides', dropping from vast heights or being turned upside down. Even if you are someone who truly enjoys this experience and gets a sense of excitement and fun from it, imagine if you were strapped into your seat for days on end, and I think you would find that the pleasurable experience would soon change.

While the sense of pleasure and increased performance produced by short-term boosts in stress hormones brought about through an increase in pressure is a valid argument, it falls down in respect of long-term stress hormone production due to the debilitating effects this causes. Individuals either do not know when to stop, or feel unable to do so because of the demands being made.

Therefore, it is important to make the distinction between 'stress' and 'pressure'. One way that you can do this is to consider the demands that are made of you in everyday life. Those demands can be internal or external. Internal demands are the ones you make of yourself: for example, if you are a perfectionist, then you make the demands of yourself, and if you make excessive demands of yourself, you are the only person who causes the stress in your life. However, some demands are external, for example, the demands that are made at work or by your family. In this case, these are external demands made of you that you have to deal with.

If the demands, whether external or internal, are matched by your resources to cope with these, then you are unlikely to feel stressed, and these are likely to fall into the domain of healthy pressure because you can deal with them. Personal resources also fall into the categories of internal and external. Internal resources relate to the way you support yourself. For example, having a healthy diet, taking regular exercise, engaging in relaxation, and a healthy thinking style will help you to deal with the demands that are made of you. External resources are those that relate to the support you get from family, friends, and colleagues, or the pleasant working environment you experience. These are things that happen to you, rather than things you have control over.

It would, therefore, be fair to say that, while pressure is good and can be a pleasurable experience if you are in control of it and you have the internal and external resources to deal with it, stress is never good. Stress means that in some way you feel you are out of control and do not have the resources you need to cope. When you are pressured, you can still feel tired, but it is a healthy tiredness, just as you might feel if you undertook a ten-mile walk. You are happy to have a bath and go to bed, but you sleep well and have enjoyed the experience, even if your muscles are a little sore the next day. However, stress is more akin to walking twenty-six miles, in the wrong shoes, and finding yourself laid up in bed for a week with all sorts of strained muscles, feeling as if the experience was far from pleasurable.

The bus journey

I have often described stress as a bus journey. You are standing at the bus stop and get on the first bus that comes along, and after a couple of stops you realize you are on the wrong bus, so you get off and then have a short walk back to your original bus stop. However, the longer you stay on the bus, the further the walk back is to where you began, and if you end up at the bus terminus, you are literally miles away. So it is with stress. Once you realize that you are experiencing stress rather than pressure, then you have a choice about what to do about it and the sooner you take action, the sooner you get back to normal. However, if you just decide to stay on the bus, or if life circumstances make it difficult for you to get off the bus, then the longer it will take you to return to normal.

WAYS THAT STRESS
CAN SHOW ITSELF

Psychological conditions that have stress associated with them

Post traumatic stress disorder (PTSD)

Post traumatic stress is often experienced following what is termed a traumatic incident. A traumatic incident is one where the person was involved in, or witnessed, an event that involved serious threat of death to a loved one or oneself. PTSD often happens when a person feels intense fear, helplessness, or a sense of horror. For many people, the feelings following a traumatic event pass within the first 4–6 weeks, often without any help. However, for some, the feelings do not pass, and may even get worse. For these people, the sense of fear leads them to avoid people, places, and things that remind them of the event. In addition, people may also experience 'flashbacks' of some aspect of the traumatic event. It is not unusual for people with PTSD to suffer from other anxiety conditions and also to experience irritability and anger.

Depression

Depression is one of the most severe of the stress-related symptoms and usually only takes effect once an individual has been experiencing stress for a considerable period of time. Most people assume that when someone is depressed they are quiet and sad, but, although this is true, there are many states associated with depression. By the time someone is so low that they may not even be able to get out of bed, they will have gone through a number of emotional stages, and depressed people can often manifest signs of irritability and anger before they become fully depressed.

Burn-out

Burn-out is the term used to describe someone who is suffering from extreme stress that tends to have built up over a period of time. As you will be aware from the stress response discussed earlier, when we perceive a threat, we produce stress hormones to deal with the situation. If a person finds him or herself exposed to stressful life situations for a prolonged period of time, a condition called burn-out can occur. Depression, anxiety, and anger are the most common emotional and psychological symptoms associated with this condition.

Life events

We all experience periods in our life when things become difficult and we face sad and stressful situations. For example, bereavement, issues surrounding infertility, financial insecurity, redundancy, etc. Such events are likely to have a whole host of challenges associated with them and, in turn, depending on our personal circumstance, a degree of stress. These situations may last for shorter or longer periods of time. However, they all pass and life continues. No one can get to their deathbed without experiencing stressful life experiences. However, the key is, wherever possible, to find ways of turning what are stressful situations into situations where we may experience pressure. It would be unrealistic not to experience concerns if you found yourself made redundant with a mortgage and no money in the bank. However, how you deal with the situation can help change it from a crisis to a period of pressure.

Frequently asked questions

Can my stress harm me?

Stress is only a term that relates to the biological stress response experienced when our brain perceives a threatening situation. This, in itself, is not harmful. However, what can be harmful is the longer-term physical, emotional, and psychological effects that continuous stress brings about. For example, even at the milder end, cortisol, as mentioned earlier, has been associated with increased appetite and it can be a contributory reason to why individuals experiencing stress often turn to comfort food, such as chocolate. If an individual overeats, and especially on those foods with little or no nutritional value but that are high in calories, weight gain is likely to take place. Depending on the amount of weight gain, this can have a negative effect on health. Additionally, there is also some research that suggests that long-term exposure can lead to organ damage, due to the effects of the stress hormones themselves. Hypertension can be associated with stress and high blood pressure is associated with strokes; add to this an individual's physical predisposition to particular medical conditions, and stress could bring about health problems.

Therefore, short-term exposure to stress is unlikely to cause much harm. However, long-term exposure is a different matter and will depend, to some extent, on an individual's own physical predispositions.

Will I have a nervous breakdown?

Stress does not cause problems like nervous breakdowns. However, if an individual goes on to develop conditions such as depression or anxiety and fails to cope with the demands being made, then it is possible, in extreme cases, that this could lead to such a breakdown.

Why do I feel so tired?

Being stressed is a tiring experience. Your body is working hard producing and coping with a range of stress hormones and their effects. It is hard to cope with life when you are stressed for any length of time. Once you are able to manage your stress, you have more energy. Although you may feel energized when you begin your stress journey, the surge of stress hormones that you produce at the time and your subsequent behaviours tire the body, and it is, therefore, not surprising that you may feel drained following periods of stress.

Additionally, even when the stress is removed, it is not uncommon for individuals to require a period of time to recover. It is often something that surprises people. They cope with a stressful time and then, when it passes and life returns to normal, they may feel unwell, get more colds/flu, and feel generally under the weather.

Stress hormones deplete the immune system, and when our immune system is run down we are far more likely to be susceptible to common ailments. When our body relaxes and begins to clear out the effects of the stress hormones, it would be naïve not to appreciate that there will be some after-effects. However, in time, these will pass as the body fully recovers.

Gladeana McMahon

Can I really learn to control my stress?

Yes, it is possible to learn to control your stress, and even to eradicate it. Once you have practised your stress management techniques, you will gain more control over your feelings, your body, and your life. Although, having said that, some people find it harder than others, and have to work harder to get their stress under control.

What about medication – isn't there a pill that will cure me?

The only real way to deal effectively in the long term with your stress is to learn to live your life differently. Some people believe that medication will help. However, apart from the fact that doctors do not prescribe tranquillizers or antidepressants for long-term use, given that they can be addictive, the problem with taking medication is that if you do not deal with the cause and change this, then the medication does not cure anything. All it does is help you manage the symptoms and provide a temporary decrease in stressful feelings, which fades once the medication is stopped.

Can alcohol help to calm me?

Using alcohol to try to calm down is counter-productive. Alcohol often exaggerates the feelings you have, and can also act as a de-inhibitor. How often have people told stories about something they said to another person that they thought better of when they were sober? Alcohol is a drug, and when we take it we alter our body and our mind. Often, when people are stressed, they turn to alcohol, cigarettes, other drugs, or food as a way of coping.

28

However, each of these can make the situation worse rather than better. As a general rule, people who are experiencing stress-related difficulties should steer well clear of alcohol or other mood-altering drugs.

BECOMING STRESS FREE

Help yourself to manage your stress

Help yourself by remembering that you can always take *some action* to minimize, even if only by a small amount, the stress you experience. This whole book is about managing stress. However, the following strategies will start you thinking about what you can begin to do to deal with stressful events, and there are further strategies at the end of this book, in the 'Stress Busting' chapter.

Come to your own aid by:

A   anticipating stressful activities and planning for them;
I   identifying the major sources of stress in your life;
D   developing a range of coping strategies that you can use on a regular basis so you become familiar with them and can call upon them when you really need them.

You can choose from the following range of techniques to suit your own preferences and circumstances.

Use your support systems

Maintain or establish a strong support network. Come to terms with your feelings and share them with others. Ask for help when you need it and accept it when it is offered. You can always offer help to other people when you are stronger and they need it. For now, it is your turn to accept help.

30

Research has shown that people with strong support networks are able to withstand the pressures of life more effectively than those who do not.

Relaxation

Relaxation can also play an important part in dealing with stress. Simple ways in which you can find time for yourself are:

- take time to enjoy a bath, light some candles, sprinkle a few drops of lavender oil into the water, and play some gentle music while you take time for yourself;
- dim the lights in the lounge, play some gentle music, close your eyes, and allow yourself time to relax;
- take some time to enjoy your garden or local park. Take time to look at all the trees and flowers.

Relaxation exercises

There are many forms of relaxation exercises, ranging from those that require physical exertion or movement to those that require nothing more than breathing or visualization techniques. Listed below are three common relaxation techniques.

BREATHING – A RESCUE REMEDY THAT CAN BE USED ANY TIME AND ANYWHERE

When you find yourself feeling stressed, or are about to deal with a difficult situation, it can be useful to have a strategy that can help you relax quickly and efficiently. The problem with many relaxation exercises is that you need to lie down or take time out, and this is impossible if you find yourself in a crowded tube train or if you are about to have a difficult meeting with your colleagues.

The following exercise provides you with a mechanism that, once you have practised it so that you can use it easily, can be called upon to help you keep calm. Keep practising until you feel confident that you would be able to undertake this breathing exercise anywhere and at any time. It is simple but effective, and can take the edge off your feelings of stress.

- Breathe in through your nose for a count of four.
- Breathe out through your mouth for a count of five.
- As you breathe out, consciously relax your shoulders.

As you breathe in and out, use your stomach muscles to control your breathing. For example, when breathing in use your stomach muscles to push out and when you breathe out use your stomach muscles to push in. This way you will breathe more deeply and this will help you gain the maximum benefit from this kind of relaxation.

DIAPHRAGMATIC BREATHING

This type of breathing is similar to the one above. However, this type of breathing exercise is one that you can use at the end of a long day as a way of unwinding.

To breathe using your diaphragm, you need to draw air into your lungs so that it will expand your stomach and not your chest. It is best to take in long, slow breaths so that you allow your body to absorb all of the oxygen you are inhaling and it is advisable to loosen belts, skirts, or anything tight that is likely to interfere with your ability to do this. It may not feel comfortable at first, simply because you are not used to this way of breathing. However, with practice you will really begin to feel the benefits of the relaxation this type of breathing exercise can offer you.

- Sit or lie comfortably and loosen your clothes.
- Put one hand on your chest and the other on your stomach.
- Inhale slowly through your nose.
- As you exhale, feel your stomach expand with your hand – if your chest expands, then concentrate more on breathing with your stomach.
- Slowly exhale through your mouth.
- Rest and repeat the exercise for between five and ten minutes

MUSCLE-TENSING EXERCISE

An American doctor, Edmund Jacobson, developed what has become known as progress muscle relaxation in the 1920s. He trained his patients to learn to voluntarily relax certain muscles in their body, and found the procedure helpful in alleviating a range of medical as well as psychological conditions. This exercise works on the premise that since muscular tension accompanies strong emotions, then you could reduce those feelings by learning how to deal with such tension.

1. Lie on the floor and make yourself comfortable.
2. Starting with your feet, tense all your muscles and then relax them. Focus on how heavy your feet feel and the way in which they are sinking into the floor.
3. Tense all the muscles in your legs as hard as you possibly can, then relax them. Focus on how heavy your

legs feel and the way in which they are sinking into the floor.

4. Move up through the other parts of your body – hips, stomach, chest, arms, neck, and face – tensing and relaxing the muscles as you go.

Note: If you suffer from high blood pressure or heart problems, you should always consult your doctor before engaging in this particular exercise.

Visualization

1. Choose a safe place to sit or lie down.
2. Imagine you are in a garden at the time of the year you like best, enjoying looking at flowers, shrubs, trees, and so on.
3. You notice a wall along one side of the garden. In the middle of the wall is an old-fashioned wooden door with a wrought iron handle on it.
4. You make your way over to the door and open it.
5. On the other side, you find yourself in your own, very special, safe place. A place no one knows about and where no one can get you.
6. Enjoy being there.
7. When you are ready, make your way back to the door.
8. Leave and shut the door firmly behind you, knowing that your special safe place is always there, whenever you choose to return there.
9. Walk around the garden and, when you are ready, open your eyes.

Note: This exercise can take between two minutes and half an hour, depending on how much time you wish to allocate to it.

Anchoring

'Anchoring' is a simple technique whereby you associate positive, calming feelings to a particular object, usually, but not always, something you wear frequently. All that is required is that in moments of difficulty you touch the chosen object, and then focus on the feelings associated with it.

1. Choose an object, say, a ring you wear all the time.
2. Now, close your eyes and focus on some aspect of your life that brings a warm glow or a smile to your face. This could be a person, place, or an activity that makes you feel good about yourself.
3. Rub the ring as you reflect on that happy thought and continue doing so for five or more minutes.
4. Wait for a few minutes and then repeat the process.
5. In carrying out this simple routine, you will have anchored positive feelings to your chosen object. From now on, merely touching that object should bring on good feelings instantly.

Meditation

Although meditation is often thought of as a component of Eastern religions, aspects of it are now being used in a new area of Cognitive–Behaviour Therapy called 'Mindfulness'. There are a number of studies that have demonstrated that engaging in regular meditation changes brainwaves, and that this has a calming effect.

Meditation describes a state of concentrated attention on some object of thought or awareness. It usually involves turning the attention inward to the mind itself. Some forms of meditation are also used alongside physical activities, such as yoga.

Biofeedback

Biofeedback involves measuring bodily responses such as blood pressure, heart rate, and skin temperature/moisture. By providing physical information to the user, it allows an individual to gain control over the physical processes that they previously thought were automatic. The popularity of biofeedback has varied since it began being used in the 1960s. However, there is now a resurgence in its use, particularly in the stress management field. Biofeedback is now being used in its most sophisticated form to help with a range of medical conditions, such as attention deficit hyperactive disorder (ADHD).

However, the simplest method, that of using what are called 'biodots' (small black dots that can be used on the skin or attached to a business card and placed between thumb and forefinger), have also been found to be helpful, as they provide the individual with information on how his or her body is reacting (i.e., whether it is manifesting the signs of stress) and, therefore, helps the person decide on the appropriate form of action to rectify the situation.

Stress and dietary tips

Stress can be made worse by taking stimulants such as tea, coffee, colas, and chocolate, all of which contain caffeine. Caffeine is a stimulant, and stimulants are best avoided when we are experiencing stress and its associated emotions. Because we produce more adrenalin when we are feeling threatened, this can affect our blood sugar levels, and they may indeed drop dramatically. Therefore, in order to keep those levels balanced, it is important to eat 'little and often' during the day. It may also be helpful to avoid refined sugars and other substances which 'give too much of a high' too quickly. Slow-release foods, such as carbohydrates (potatoes, pasta, rice, bread, apples, and bananas) are a much better idea, as they fuel the body in a more even, controlled way. See the Stress-Free Diet section (p. 174) for further information on how you can support your stress management strategies through diet.

Managing your time

Learn to manage your time as effectively as possible. Time is a valuable commodity. How many times do you catch yourself saying, *'I'd really like to but I don't have the time'*, or *'There just aren't enough hours in the day'*? Too much activity leads to exhaustion, too little and we become bored and frustrated. There are 168 hours in a week, and 8,736 hours in a 365-day year, and so, with a finite amount of time, it is important that we make the most of what we have. Many people who experience stress find that poor time management is a factor in their lives. In such instances, when the person may have been working far too hard, it only take one simple thing to go wrong, such as the printer running out of toner, to send that individual into a fit of anger. In addition, if an individual feels that he or she does not have enough time to enjoy life, but is always running around for others or trying to keep on top of a never-ending workload, this, too, can tip the balance into a stressful response. See the 'Time Management' section on p. 46 for further information on how to use time effectively.

Gladeana McMahon

Sleep

It is important for a person's psychological and physiological well-being to get adequate sleep. Sleep is essential for survival, health, and fitness, and research suggests that it is the quality of sleep that is most important. However, too little or too much may lead to poor performance. The amount of sleep required varies considerably from person to person. Most people sleep for seven hours; some may need nine, and others only five. Ironically, it is often worry about losing sleep that produces more negative symptoms than the loss of sleep itself. Many people underestimate the amount of sleep they actually get due to the amount of time they spend worrying about not sleeping when they are awake.

The kind of sleep that is most important is what is called REM, or Rapid Eye Movement, sleep, which is linked to dreaming. All people dream, even if they wake without any memory of dreaming.

Stress is one of the main causes of sleep disturbance. Many people lie awake at night worrying about problems, or thinking about the future in an anxious manner; then, having finally fallen asleep, awake feeling tired as the original worries are still there.

If you are experiencing difficulties sleeping, it can help to:

- ensure you have a routine. Have a warm milky drink, as milk contains tryptophan, which promotes sleep;
- take a warm bath. Using relaxing bath oils may also help;
- avoid sleeping during the day

38

- avoid drinking caffeine, as caffeine is a stimulant and may keep you awake. Too much coffee during the day could still affect you in the evening;
- avoid a heavy meal and eating late at night;
- ensure that you get plenty of exercise during the day. It may be particularly helpful to take your exercise during the late afternoon or early evening;
- use your relaxation exercises as outlined above;
- ensure your sleeping environment is as pleasant as possible, not too hot or too cold. Switch off electrical appliances to avoid a 'mains hum'.
- turn the clock away from you. Research has shown that turning the clock away from you helps if you are having problems sleeping, as clock watching is liable to keep you awake, whereas not knowing what the time is encourages you to sleep more.

If you are not sleeping because of a traumatic event, you may also need to feel secure in your sleeping space. For example, ensure that all doors and windows have proper locks and are alarmed.

Some people find that changing the position of the bed, or rearranging the layout of the bedroom, can be helpful, as can be removing objects such as pictures or ornaments which may seem frightening in a half-awake state. Introducing pleasant smells may also create a pleasant atmosphere. Lavender oil is particularly popular, and recommended by complementary health practitioners such as aromatherapists to aid relaxation and sleep.

If you find yourself unable to sleep within forty-five minutes of going to bed, then get up and engage in another activity, such as reading. After 20–25 minutes, go back to bed again and try to get some sleep. Repeat the process if you still have not fallen asleep for as long as is necessary. It is important that your bed remains associated with sleeping. Some people find it better to avoid getting up, as they say that once they are up and engaged in another activity, they are wide awake. If this sounds more like you, then stay in bed and engage in the breathing exercise listed above. Although you may not fall back to sleep quickly, your body will be more relaxed.

People may experience nightmares following a traumatic incident. If this is the case it can be helpful to:

- write down the dream in the third person (*Jane could not get away*), then in the first person tense (*I could not get away*) until you feel more comfortable with the dream;
- think about what the dream might mean. Is it an actual replay, rather like a flashback, of the traumatic inciden,t or is the dream completely different?
- think about how you could change the story. For example, if you were trapped, perhaps you could find a way out or a sudden surge of strength to remove the item trapping you. Practise this new version of the dream in your imagination while you are awake;
- practised your new version of the dream again when you are tired and relaxed and before going to sleep;
- tell yourself that you intend to replace the dream with the new ending the next time it happens.

You may find you have to repeat this exercise before it becomes fully effective. It would be helpful to keep a note using the 0–8 scale of the emotional distress experienced as a result of each nightmare. You may find that if the nightmares do not stop, they may change in degrees of severity, and by keeping a note of this, you can see how your nightmares are weakening.

Physical exercise

As mentioned earlier, physical exercise has a number of positive benefits. It improves blood flow to your brain, bringing additional sugars and oxygen that may be needed to aid thinking. When you are thinking, the brain can build up a kind of waste product that, in time, can cloud your thinking ability. Exercise increases blood and oxygen flow to the brain and helps to clear out the waste products. In addition, exercise causes the release of chemicals called endorphins into your bloodstream. These give you a feeling of happiness and overall well-being. There is evidence that physically fit people cope better when under pressure than those who are not.

Stress at work

Most people these days would say that they have far too much work to do, working unreasonably long hours in an attempt to stay on top of the workload. *Doing things for any length of time means you run the risk of becoming exhausted.*

To do a good job, you need to understand what is expected and, by understanding the priorities in your job, you can focus on these activities and minimize work on other tasks as much as possible. This helps you to keep your workload under control.

Undertaking a Job Analysis can be a useful technique to cut through clutter and distraction to help you see what you need to do.

The following steps will help you:

1. *Assess your documentation.*
   Look at your job description. Identify the key objectives and priorities within it and find out if there is any training available.
2. *Organizational culture and strategy.*
   What is your organization's mission statement? Make sure you understand the tasks that contribute to the strategy. Organizations also have their own culture, and it is helpful for you to understand this. What type of an organization is it, what values does it subscribe to? Check that your way of working is consistent with your organization's mission statement and the company culture.
3. *Who is seen as the best and why?*
   There may be people similar to you working in the organization and some may be more successful. If this is the case, then stand back and ask yourself why this is, what do they do that you do not.
4. *People and resources.*
   The next step is to check that you have the staff support, resources, and training needed to do an excellent job. If this is not the case, then it will not matter how long or hard you work; you cannot achieve all that you would either like to or that the organization may want you to. Be realistic, but most of all be honest with yourself.
5. *Talking to the boss.*
   It is important that you talk to your manager and

ensure that s/he realizes that you want to do your best and will seek guidance when necessary to do so. However, it is also important that s/he is aware when the demands being made of you are not achievable.

Additional strategies that could be of help to you are the following.

- Set a realistic schedule. Analyse your schedule, responsibilities, and daily tasks. Find a balance between work and family life. Find time for your social activities and 'downtime', too.
- Do not over-commit. We often underestimate how long things will take. If you've got too much on your shoulders, drop tasks that are not truly necessary to the bottom of the list or eliminate them entirely.
- Get to work a bit earlier. Ten minutes can make the difference between feeling at ease or ending up feeling rushed. Do not add to your stress levels by running late.
- Take regular breaks. Make sure to take short breaks throughout the day to sit back and clear your mind. Get away from your desk for lunch, even if for only twenty minutes, as this will help you recharge and make you more, not less, productive.
- Small steps. If a project seems too big, break it down into small, manageable steps and do not try to take on everything at once.
- Get others to help. At home or at work, ask for help and do not be a martyr. Let go of the need to control everything and you will be helping yourself let go of unnecessary stress.

Managing change

As you saw earlier, stress involves a complex relationship between the demands made of a person and the personal and external resources he or she has to meet these demands. These demands can trigger the stress response, as outlined on p. 8.

The demands that are made of you could be 'internal'; that is, your own thinking style. Perfectionists put pressure on themselves and this is, therefore, an internal demand, as no one else is making it. Resources comprise factors such as your physical health, financial security, social and family support. Keep a balance so that you do not have more demands than resources to deal with them. If demands exceed your resources, you may feel you cannot cope, and this is the beginning of what has become known as stress.

Some people talk about healthy and unhealthy stress, meaning that some stress is good for you. As mentioned earlier, it is easier to think in terms of the idea of 'pressure' and 'stress'. Pressure is healthy and something that can motivate you. Some people love to live in a pressured way with lots of deadlines and things to do. The distinction between pressure and stress is that you experience pressure when you have the resources you need to deal with the demands being made of you. Pressure turns to stress when the pressure becomes too great, lasts too long, comes suddenly, and ends up with you feeling it cannot be controlled.

Stress is a very personal matter. A situation that might stress your friend may not affect you, and vice versa. An event may have proved stressful to you at one point in your life, but you may have developed additional resources to deal with the situation as you have grown older.

Work can be a great source of stress – time pressures, excessive workload, poor relations with colleagues/ managers, poor communications within your organization, being exposed to continual change, not being trained to do the job, and job insecurity all play their part. Stress can be experienced in your personal life – family problems, life changes/crises, increasing demands between home and work-all may affect us.

In 1967, Thomas Holmes and Richard Rahe, two American psychologists, first published a scale of forty-three life events considered to be stressful. Each event was scored according to the degree of stress associated with the activity. the table below lists the top seven items, together with the score associated with each event.

The life event	Score
Death of a partner	100
Divorce	73
Marital separation	65
Imprisonment	63
Death of a close family member	63
Personal illness or injury	53
Marriage	50

In addition to the above, other items included:

- dealing with Christmas;
- pregnancy;
- sexual difficulties;
- legal action;

- moving house;
- changing school or college;
- change in living conditions;
- change in hours or working conditions;
- arguments with partners or family;
- adoption or birth of a child.

One of the advantages of understanding the impact of life events is that it can help you anticipate stressful events. For example, knowing that having a baby can be stressful allows you to consider what stress management techniques are likely to help you. A fact that surprised many people was that life events seen as pleasurable also carried a stress rating: for example, getting married, having a baby or gaining a promotion. Good experiences usually entail a degree of change, and it can be the changes to lifestyle and the need to develop new coping skills that contribute to the stress experienced.

Time management

If you are unable to manage your time effectively, you will not follow through on the promises to improve your life that you make to yourself. You might find yourself wanting and wishing things to be different, but saying you do not have enough time to practise your new skills. Many stressed individuals often cite time management as one of their biggest challenges.

Time is a valuable commodity, too much activity leads to exhaustion; too little and you could become bored and frustrated.

EXERCISE

To help you consider your time management needs, think about the activities you are involved in on a weekly basis and list these in a copy of the table below.

ITEM	TIME ALLOCATION
e.g., Work commitments, travel, family, etc.	

How effectively do you allocate your time?

ASK YOURSELF THE FOLLOWING QUESTIONS:

1. Do I have time to do what   Yes   N o
   I would like to?
2. Do I put off activities because   Yes   N o
   I have too much to do?

3. Do I feel there simply is   Yes   N o
    not enough time?
4. Have I ever thought about the   Yes   N o
    way I use my time?
5. Am I happy about the way   Yes   N o
    I allocate my time?

If you have answered yes to 2 and 3 and no to 1, 4, and 5 you might need to consider how you allocate your time and whether this is effective for you.

Time can be divided into six areas, and it may be helpful to draw a circle, labelling this your 'Time Allowance Pie' (Figure 3). Consider each of the six areas below and divide your pie into the portions that you believe accurately represents your allocation of time over a one-week period.

Work time   Time earmarked for work, paid or voluntary.
Home time   Time for housework/maintenance, personal care, and gardening.
Other time   Time for family, friends, and children.
'Me' Time   Time for hobbies, relaxation, exercise, and sleep.
'Us' time   Time to spend with our partner
Quiet time   Time to ourselves for thinking, evaluating, and reflecting (e.g., *how well you are doing at your learning to be your own life coach*).

If you are not happy with the amount of time you have allocated to any activity, consider how to reallocate the time you have so that you achieve the balance you are seeking. If there are slices of your pie that are greatly out

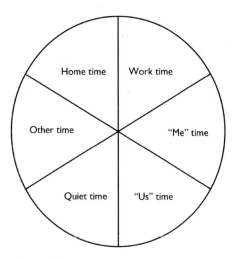

Figure 3.   Time allocation pie

of balance, you may find it helpful to keep a written record of your feelings about how you have allocated your time over a one-week period.

Apart from completing the time allocation pie you could also consider:

1.   How you manage your time.
2.   How you fritter your time away.
3.   How you could be more effective in managing your time.
4.   How you could make more time to do the things you like.
5.   How you could do less of the things you dislike.

At the end of a week you should have a better idea of how you spend your time and what you would like to create more or less time to do.

Gladeana McMahon

Your biological clock has an effect on time management, as there are times of the day when you will feel more alert than others. For example, some people prefer mornings, when they feel full of energy, but find they feel exhausted mid-afternoon. If this is the case, it makes sense to try, wherever possible, to save your difficult tasks for the time of the day when you have most energy. Your best time of day is often called your 'prime time'.

Consider other people's 'prime time', as there may be times of the day when it would be better to approach certain people. If there are times of the day when you are more energetic, why not seek out such times in others, as this may help influence a positive outcome.

There are three aspects of time management to consider:

- checklists and notes as ways of keeping track of the work you have to do;
- calendars and appointment books for planning ahead;
- short-, medium-, and long-term goal setting and the recognition of your personal values and desires.

Poor organization

Poor organization leads to an increase in stress and can mean

- poorly maintained filing system (e.g., *filing not done on a regular basis*). Valuable time can be lost looking for information;
- no system to identify relevant information (e.g., *papers and documentation simply thrown into a pile*);
- indiscriminately keeping everything that is received, filling valuable space as well as using time to locate items – the 'just in case' principle.

50

If you find yourself spending time on non-productive discussions either at work or with friends when you need to be doing something else, consider the following:

- keep conversations short;
- keep a clock nearby to remind you to deal with the call effectively;
- learn how to use the three-step model of assertiveness:

    Step 1: I understand your problem, e.g., *'I do appreciate you need to speak soon'*;

    Step 2: However, I think or feel, e.g., *'However, I am back to back with meetings'*;

- Step 3: and I suggest, e.g., *'and I suggest we put a call in the diary for the end of the week'*.

Diaries, personal and electronic organizers

A diary or an electronic organizer are mechanisms to keep track of appointments and are good for planning ahead. If you use a diary or personal organizer you may also find it useful to mark your appointments in pencil, as this allows them to be changed with the minimum of fuss. If you choose to use an electronic organizer, you need to back up your data on a regular basis to protect against loss of information.

To do lists

A 'to-do' list is a form of memory aid. In addition to recording tasks to be done, a simple system such as A, B, and C can be used as a way of organizing priorities.

A = Urgent items which require immediate attention.

B = Important items which require attention in the near future.

C = Non-essential or non-urgent items.

Post-it notes

Some people find it helpful to place post-it notes in full view to remind them to carry out urgent tasks.

Filing systems

A portable lockable metal filing system can prove useful to help you store household documentation. Being able to find something first time can really save you time.

Effective time management means thinking about what you do, how you do it, and how you can make the most of this finite resource. Unlike most items, time cannot be stored for future use.

To ensure you use your time effectively, you need to build in 'Quiet' time as a legitimate activity. This type of activity enables you to evaluate the present while considering the future.

Learning to be grateful

Learning to create a balanced view of life can boost a sense of well-being by balancing out the positive against the more challenging aspects. Learning to recognize and appreciate the good things in your life is a key to creating just such a balance. There is now a growing body of evidence that demonstrates that people who focus on what they are grateful for are not only happier, but more resilient too, and less likely to experience stress.

The gratitude visit

One exercise that can be used to do this is called 'The Gratitude Visit'.

1. Think of someone in your life whom you feel grateful to and write that person a letter, describing what they have done and how this has had an impact on you.
2. Once you have completed your letter, contact the person concerned and arrange to meet with them. When you are with them, tell them that you have something you would like to say and then read out your letter. At the end, you can give the person the letter you have written as a gift.

Many people feel embarrassed at the idea of undertaking such an exercise. However, this has more to do with the way we have been brought up. By facing your embarrassment you will find that the other person is moved by what you have said, and that this sharing of positive experiences enhances the relationship.

You could, of course, just send the letter, but if you do so you will miss the moment of shared experience.

Your grateful list

Another exercise that can be used to help you discover the good things is the 'grateful list'.

1. Write down everything in life you are grateful for, both in the past as well as the present. As you see your list grow, you begin to realize that life is made up of good and bad and that there are always things to be grateful for.
2. Your list needs to include things people have said and done as well as the things that you count as good. Many of these things may be small, such as being able to see the flowers bloom in spring.

53

Every item is something for you to focus on that you recognize provides you with pleasure. It is worth doing this exercise at least once every three months to really capture the good things in your life.

Linked with gratitude is the ability to recognize on a more regular basis the things in life that you are grateful for and that bring you a sense of satisfaction or joy.

The blessings exercise

The art of creating a balanced and more optimistic and positive view on life means learning to recognize yourself and others at their best.

1. Each night for one week, look back on the day and identify the things that have gone well for you. They do not have to be impressively meaningful; they could simply be the recognition that 'I enjoyed watching the children play in the park'.
2. Write down everything you can think of and consider your role in what happened. When you write something down this helps you focus on the event in question, and focusing on your part in the event helps you to gain confidence and feel a sense of control in your life.

This exercise is aimed at helping you become more aware and create a balanced view of your life while increasing your sense of confidence and control. However, it is possible to overdo it. For example, if you tackle this exercise in such a way that it becomes a chore and something you 'have to do', rather than something you want to do. It is not about how much you manage to identify, it is about the quality of what the events mean to you. Better to have three meaningful items than spend your time competitively looking for things to include.

Getting the most from life

The following exercises are all aimed at helping you get the most from your life as, by doing so, you are also stress-proofing yourself.

Creating a wonderful day

Making the most of your life and taking time to enjoy being with the people you care about helps you develop psychological resilience. It is also good stress management, and helps to build and maintain good relationships.

1. Think about the type of day that you would like to design for someone close to you. It could be a family member, your partner, or a friend. Think about the things that you both like doing and that are important to you.
2. Take time to think about how you would like the day to be, what to include, where you will go, and the things you will do.
3. Invite the person concerned and decide on when this activity will take place.
4. When the day comes, take time during it to enjoy what you are doing and savour the time you have.
5. At the end of your day, before you go to bed, sit back and reflect on what you did, the things you enjoyed,

and how good it was to spend time with the person concerned.

Me at my best

When you think about you at your best, your feelings of confidence and well-being increase and, if you act as if you are something, the likelihood is that you will develop the associated behaviours. This exercise helps you get in touch with the best in yourself and helps you build greater optimism.

1. Think about how you would like to be. Imagine what it would be like to be the way you desire. What would you be doing? What would you be saying to other people? How would you be feeling? What would others notice about you? Create the image of you as a fully functioning person living your life to the best.
2. There may have been times in your life where you felt like this and, if so, recapture the thoughts and feelings you experienced.
3. At least three times a week for four weeks, note down your experience of you at your best. Imagine that the things you desire have happened and how you feel about this. The more positively you can write about your feelings, the better.

Identifying your strengths

When you feel stressed, it is all too easy to forget that you are a person with strengths. However, if you can recognize your strengths, not only will this remind you that you can cope, but it will also encourage you to use your strengths to overcome difficult situations.

Complete the following sentence

Sentence completion is a technique you can use to aid your self-understanding and self awareness. The essence of the sentence completion exercise is to start with an incomplete sentence and keep adding different endings. This exercise can help you identify your strengths and help you uncover some that you did not realize you had. This exercise asks you to complete the sentences in each box with at least one ending, but ideally as many endings that you can imagine.

For example, I am someone who can . . .

I am someone who can succeed when I set my mind to something

STRENGTHS SENTENCE COMPLETION EXERCISE

1. Creativity and judgement

Strength	Characteristics
Creativity/originality/ingenuity	I am creative when I . . . I am creative when I . . .
Judgement/open mindedness/cal thinking	I am non-judgemental criti-when I . . . I use my critical thinking skills when I . . .
Curiosity/interest/openness to experience/novelty-seeking	I am using my curiosity when I . . . I am open to experiences when I . . .
Love of learning	I demonstrate my love of learning when I . . . I am open to finding out about new things when I . . .

(continued)

57

Perspective	I am open to seeing other people's perspectives when I . . .
	I am able to share my thoughts with other when I . . .

2. Courage	
Strength	Characteristic
Bravery/valour	I am brave when I . . .
	I have stood by my beliefs when . . .
Industry/perseverance/diligence	I have stuck at things when I I managed to overcome problems and completed a task when I . . .
Integrity/honesty/authenticity	I took responsibility for myself when I faced . . .
	I was true to myself when I . . .
Vitality/zest/enthusiasm	I find life an adventure when I . . .
	I am full of enthusiasm and energy when I . . .

3. Love	
Strength	Characteristic
Intimacy/reciprocal attachment	I am able to form close relationships because I . . .
	I believe I have people in my . . .
Kindness/generosity/nurturance	I look after others when I . . .
	I try to do favours for people because I . . .
Social intelligence/ emotional intelligence/ personal intelligence	I am good socially because I . . .
	I understand other people because I . . .

(*continued*)

4. *Justice*

Strengths	Characteristics
Citizenship/loyalty/teamwork	I help out my community because I . . . I am loyal to people when I . . .
Equity/fairness	I am fair to others when I . . . I manage difficult situations well when I . . .
Leadership	I take the lead when I . . . I help other people get things done when I . . .

5. *Temperance*

Strengths	Characteristics
Forgiveness/mercy	I am able to forgive people because . . . I am able to accept my shortcomings when I . . .
Modesty/humility	I am happy for others to get the attention because . . . I don't need to seek recognition because . . .
Prudence/caution	I don't take unnecessary risks because I . . . I am careful in dealing with others because I . . .
Self-control/self-regulation	I am able to wait for things because I . . . I am able to be self-disciplined when I . . .

6. *Transcendence*

Strengths	Characteristics
Awe/wonder/appreciation of beauty and excellence	I am able to appreciate the beauty in life when I . . . I am able to appreciate excellence when I see it because . . . *(continued)*

Gratitude	I am thankful for my life because I . . .
	I show my thanks to people when I . . .
Hope/optimism/ future-mindedness	I believe that the best can be achieved because I . . .
	I can influence a positive outcome when I . . .
Playfulness/humour	I am playful when I . . .
	I tend to laugh when I . . .
Spirituality/sense of purpose/ faith/religiousness	I see meaning and purpose in life when I . . .
	I believe that I am here for a purpose because . . .

Now that you have completed as many sentences as you can, go back and look at these. Which ones surprised you? Which ones were difficult and why? Are there any areas that you think you would like to develop and why?

This exercise should provide you with insight into your behaviour and your thinking processes.

You may find it helpful to visit www.authentichappi-ness.sas.upenn.edu, as there are a number of questionnaires that you can complete on a range of aspects from identifying your personal strengths to increasing your resilience.

What is my purpose?

There is a strong relationship between your sense of purpose or meaning in life and how well you deal with stress. Positive Psychology focuses on helping individuals to identify their individual values, helping individuals discover their own sense of purpose and meaning.

1. Think about times in your life that have given you the greatest sense of satisfaction. Go back to that time and remember what you were doing, who you were doing it with, what was happening, and how you felt. Alternatively, think about a time when you were so engrossed in what you were doing that time sped by more quickly than you thought. Again, think about what you were doing, who was there, why this was so engrossing, and how you felt.

2. You will need a paper and pen, or you could open a Word document and use your computer. Start by writing down the first sentence, 'My Purpose in Life is . . .', and write down anything that comes into your mind.

3. Rate your feelings on a scale of 0–10, 0 = not much feeling and 10 = deep, meaningful feelings, such as joy. When you have completed this part of the exercise, go back over your list and see how many items elicited such feelings and ask yourself why they were so meaningful.

This exercise will help you begin to identify those aspects in your life that are related to your sense of meaning and purpose. Once you have an idea about what they are, you can do more of these or think of activities that are similar and can add to the ones you already have.

Being kind helps me as much as it does you

As you might imagine, given the title of this exercise, it is about doing something for someone else with no other motive in mind than being kind and doing a good deed for its own sake. In some ways, it is the smaller acts of kindness that may leave more of an impression on someone than dreaming up larger ones. It is not that larger acts do not matter, but that life is usually made up of smaller acts of thoughtfulness.

Doing something for someone else not only brightens up life for the other person, it makes you feel better in the process. The more acts you can carry out each day, the better and the more pay-off for you as well as others.

1. Think about the kinds of acts you might do for:

    Those close to you

●   Take someone out who you know finds this difficult – say an elderly relative.
●   Take an evening meal round to someone who has just come out of hospital or may be feeling unwell.
●   What other acts can you think of?

    For society

●   Give blood on a regular basis.
●   Give your old clothes to charity.
●   What other acts can you think of?

    For individuals you do not know

●   If you have time left on your parking ticket, give the ticket to another motorist.
●   Help someone who is struggling with a child's push-chair down the stairs at the local tube station .
●   What other acts can you think of?

Many of my clients have taken on voluntary work and found that this boosted their sense of well-being. For example, one client helped out over the Christmas period at the shelter that was set up by the charity 'Crisis'. He was pretty stressed at the time and feeling very hard done by. As he was single he decided to volunteer. When I saw him post Christmas, his mood was much improved. He found the experience uplifting as well as humbling. He still had to deal with the problems he was experiencing, but said that he was grateful to have had the experience of volunteering and that what he saw and did put his life back into perspective.

STRESS-FREE THINKING

The four stages of change

Whenever you learn something new, regardless of whether it is a practical skill such as using the Internet, or a mental skill such as changing behaviour or negative beliefs, you go through a set sequence of learning:

- stage one, unconsciously incompetent;
- stage two, consciously incompetent;
- stage three, consciously competent;
- stage four, unconsciously competent.

This process is known as Robinson's Four Stages of Learning

Stage 1: Unconsciously incompetent

'*Don't know it and can't do it.*'
You feel unhappy but have no idea why.

Stage 2: Consciously incompetent

'*I begin to notice just how often I have negative thoughts but I don't seem able to change anything.*'
During this stage, you become aware of what is happening but seem unable to do anything about it. This is the awareness stage: for example, realizing the ways in which you make yourself feel stressed by magnifying situations in a negative way, but not being able to stop.

Stage 3: Consciously competent

'*I have skills and can handle situations better although I still have to think about what I am doing.*'

You now have a range of strategies to use, but you still have to think about what you are doing, as it does not feel natural.

Stage 4: Unconsciously competent

'*I suddenly realized what I had done and how I handled the situation without even thinking about it.*'

The more you practise your new skills, the more your behaviour feels 'natural'. You are now working off your automatic pilot – doing things without thinking about them.

Change happens over time, and it is persistence, practice, and the belief in taking one small step at a time that wins the day.

The role of optimism

Optimists think more positively about life, seeing the good in situations and minimizing the bad. Pessimists think that optimists are foolish and optimists think that pessimists are depressing. Researchers believe that optimism and pessimism have a genetic factor. However, there is also evidence to suggest that it is the environment we are brought up in that shapes the way we think. We discussed earlier in the book the way that behaviours can be learnt, and this is true for optimists and pessimists. However, optimistic people are more likely to be more resilient and less likely to experience stress. When they do, they are more likely to take action and deal with the situation more effectively.

There is research to suggest that there are advantages to being an optimist. For example, it would appear that optimists live longer, achieve more, and have happier lives.

When you suffer from stress, it can be hard to believe that you can ever become more optimistic about life. However, it is possible to relearn behaviours and ways of thinking. The following exercise will help you begin this process.

EXERCISE

Situations where you experience optimism and pessimism

1. Name two people you feel more optimistic around and state why.

    (i) _____

    (ii) _____

2. Identify two situations that you have felt more optimistic about and state why.

    (i) _____

    (ii) _____

3. Name two people you feel pessimistic around and state why.

    (i) _____

    (ii) _____

4. Identify two recent situations where you have felt pessimistic and state why.

    (i) _____

    (ii) _____

When you look at your answers can you spot any patterns forming? For example, are you more optimistic with certain people but pessimistic with others?

Pessimism drains you. However, pessimistic thinking can be changed. Changing your thinking style is perfectly possible if you are prepared to put in some time and effort.

A third group has been identified: those who plan for the worst or devise a fall-back position if things don't work out as hoped. They never believe anything good will automatically happen. However, they do put themselves forward even though they do not believe they will succeed. They work hard and prepare. These are called 'Defensive Pessimists'. Defensive pessimism seems to work for some people. If you have a go you are probably a defensive pessimist – if you don't you are a pessimist.

The following exercise is aimed at helping you begin the process of increasing your optimistic outlook on life.

EXERCISE

Ways of improving optimism

1. Make a list of three good things that have happened to you at the end of each day. The things you list do not have to be major items, but simply tasks you may feel you have handled better than you thought you would.

2. When you find yourself looking at life pessimistically, replace your negative thought with a positive thought or image.

3. Make a list of positive statements and repeat these to yourself on a daily basis (e.g., *'I can learn to think and behave differently'*).

Are my thoughts real?

We try to make sense of the world around us; we interpret the messages we receive and use these to decide on the best ways of coping with our environment. Sometimes what we think is not really what is happening. There is often more than one way to look at a situation. The way we see the world shapes what we do. Once we realize this, we have more choices about the way we behave and can make better decisions.

Look at Figure 4. Is it a Native American, or is it a member of the Inuit people?

Perhaps you can see only one image. This exercise is rather like life. Often, we do not see what is right in front of our eyes and, even when it is pointed out, it can be hard to change our viewpoint. Time, patience, and a little effort can work wonders.

Figure 4. A Native American – or a member of the Inuit people?

How do my beliefs affect me?

Since the 1950s, psychologists have identified a number of beliefs that people apply to their everyday living. In the trauma field, the three 'life beliefs', which have been identified as being crucial to the speed at which a person can recover from a traumatic incident, are:

- bad things happen to other people;
- life has meaning and purpose;
- I would always do the right thing in an emergency.

All of these beliefs cause their own particular type of problems. For example, bad things *don't* just happen to 'other people' – they can happen to *anyone*. Someone has to be a statistic and *bad things happen to good people and good people sometimes do bad things.*

If you believe that 'life has meaning and purpose', then person-made disasters, acts of cruelty, or senseless bloodshed are more likely to be greatly disturbing. Such incidents seem meaningless and with no purpose. In such circumstances, then, an individual may feel very frightened, especially if he or she had always believed that life did have meaning and purpose. In these cases, depending on the individual concerned, it can either add to or reduce the stress we feel.

For those who believe they would 'do the right thing' in an emergency, this belief can become challenged when they find themselves behaving in a different way to the way they would have predicted. When this is the case, the individual may experience more stress, based on the internal demands the individual makes of him/herself in relation to whether the individual believes that s/he should have behaved differently.

69

As mentioned earlier, some of these involuntary and uncontrollable reactions are pre-programmed by our biology. When we are in a life-threatening situation, our stress response kicks in and our body becomes like an alarm system. Either we flee to escape danger, or we stay and stand our ground. Either way, it is almost impossible for anyone to predict with any accuracy how he/she will behave in a life-threatening situation.

Human beings tend to use beliefs to guide everyday transactions. For example, '*I will go to work and come home safely*', or '*I will travel on the bus quite safely*'. We may find our thinking becomes distorted if our beliefs are challenged by life events that, in turn, can cause us to become hyper-aroused and hyperactive. Anxiety can be a common feature of such thinking, and such feelings are stressful.

People who experience anger often have beliefs along the lines of '*People must treat me fairly*'; '*If you don't show people that you are strong then they will take advantage*'; '*People are out to get you*'; '*I have to stand up for myself otherwise no one else will*'. If we hold such beliefs, then we may well experience more stress in our lives.

As mentioned earlier, beliefs are formed from the messages we receive as children from those around us. It is these messages that shape the way we think about ourselves.

Faulty thinking

There is a considerable amount of research that demonstrates a link between stress and the way we think. Let's look at the relationship between stress and thinking style by considering two people, Matt and Lucy, who are waiting to be interviewed and where the interviewers are running late.

Lucy might recognize that this is not an uncommon situation and takes the time to go over in her mind all the achievements she has had in her current and past jobs, what she does well, and what she can bring to the job should she get it. Matt sits there and starts thinking that the interviewers must like the person they are interviewing, otherwise they would not be overrunning; he then starts to thinks there may be little point in being interviewed, after all, if they like the person they are seeing, then maybe he does not stand a chance. Both experience the same situation, but the way they think about it either helps them or hinders. It is not rocket science to work out who will be in the best position to interview well.

Faulty thinking relates to how we interpret situations and the following considers the ways in which we can change our thinking to that which is likely to be more effective in dealing with stress.

A good way of thinking about whether your thoughts, feelings, and associated behaviours are reasonable is to ask yourself if everyone in your situation would think, act, and feel in the same way. For example, if others might deal with a situation differently, it is possible for you to do so, and it is likely that all that is different is the way the other person thinks about what has happened. If there are alternative perspectives, and if such alternatives would provide you with better outcomes, then it is possible for you to learn to think in a more productive manner.

Healthy thinking

Simple as ABC

There is a model used in Cognitive–Behavioural Therapy called the ABC model (see Table 3). The following

Gladeana McMahon

Table 3.   ABC model

A Situation (trigger)	B Thoughts based on beliefs	C Consequences
Waiting to be interviewed	**Thoughts** *They must really like the person they are seeing; probably no point in my being here.*	**Feelings** Anxiety/stress
	Beliefs *I"m not as bright as other people so I have to woirk harder, but others will always. come out on top.*	**Actions** Becoming tense, stomach tightening, and breathing becoming more laboured.

describes how situations trigger thoughts, how thoughts trigger feelings, and how feelings lead to actions.

Triggers

It will be helpful to you if you can begin to identify the kinds of situations that trigger your stress. Once you have identified these, you can go on to consider whether the way you think about the situation is the cause of your stress and how you can go about changing the way that you think.

For the following exercise, make a list of all the situations that you can identify where you become more stressed. If you find this a difficult exercise to complete, you may find it useful to prefix your situation with the words – 'I feel stressed when . . .'

EXERCISE

I feel stressed when . . .

1.

2.

3.

4.

5.

6.

7.

8.

9.

10.

Keeping a stress diary

Some of you may have found the above exercise quite easy and others may have found it quite hard. However, it is important to be able to identify the situations that cause you the greatest difficulty so that you can develop the appropriate counter-measures to eliminate or reduce your stress and any unhelpful actions you then engage in.

A stress diary is a useful tool to keep track of what is happening, what triggers your stress, and how you react. It is a way of identifying situations and what you did at the time, as this way you can build a picture of how you react and respond to your environment. Once you can identify the situations to which you respond in a stressful way, you are halfway to being able to do something about your behaviour.

It is best to write down the incidents in your diary as soon after they have happened as possible and to make your accounts of what happened as full as possible.

When you have completed your diary, read over what you have written and try to understand what it was about the situation in question that caused you to feel stressed. Once you have done this, then consider alternative ways in which you could have behaved.

For example, let's look at the entries in Will's diary (see Table 4). In the first situation, Will is thinking about returning to university as a mature student to undertake a law degree. He is due to attend an interview for the course and, because he is much older than the other hopefuls and the course is a popular one, he is worried that he will be disadvantaged.

There are various ways in which Will could handle this situation either to minimize his stress levels or to eradicate them completely.

1. He could focus on the fact that being a mature student could be seen more favourably as he has more life experience than the other hopefuls.
2. He could listen to his iPod to distract himself, thinking about all the good things that he has achieved in his life so far.
3. He could tell himself that even if he was not successful, there are other courses and that attending the interview will be a learning experience that he could

Table 4. *Will's stress diary*

Date	Time	Situation (trigger)	What I did
10.1.10	10.30 a.m.	On train to university where I am about to be interviewed for a place on the law degree course I really want to do. annoyed me.	Feeling anxious and very stressed. I am so much older than the other students and they are likely. to be better equipped than I am as they are just out of school.

use to help him secure a place at another university if he were not successful.

Once you have identified the kinds of situations that trigger your stress, what you do in these situations, and the kinds of thoughts that go through your head, you will gain not just an understanding, but also have the option of devising strategies (behaviours and alternative ways of thinking about what has happened) so that you can mini-mize or totally eradicate your stress.

Do remember that there is a difference between a natural sense of concern and feeling stressed. If we want something, then, a bit like an actor who may experience a few first night nerves, you may feel some concern and/or nervousness, as that would be quite normal. However, there is a big difference between a few butterflies in the stomach and full-on fear or stress. The first is likely to help you and make you more alert but not stressed, whereas the second is more likely to cause you to become much more stressed than is good for you and probably lead you to feel anxiety. As anxiety tends to block our ability to think clearly, this means that you actually disadvantage yourself in the process as well as experience stressful feelings.

Negative thoughts

Much of our thinking is in the form of automatic thoughts. We use the term automatic as we are often not even aware that we are thinking them. These thoughts simply seem to 'pop' into our head. In a way, it is rather like supermarket music – something in the background of which we are not really aware.

Negative automatic thoughts are often referred to as NATs. In many ways this is a good description for such thoughts, since, rather like the insects, they are irritating. Although you do not often see them, their bite can irritate for days. These kinds of thoughts are usually distorted – that is to say, they do not match the facts. They are involuntary and difficult to switch off.

As we have had many years to perfect our thinking style, it can be hard to change the way we think. If you have ever tried to break a habit, you will appreciate how hard it can be.

The role of judgements

When a situation occurs, you form a judgement about what has happened. Your thoughts about what has happened tell you that this was either, a good thing, an 'all right' thing, or a bad thing, and it is these judgements of situations that may help or hinder you when it comes to managing your stress.

For example, if Will keeps on thinking that he is disadvantaged and about all the negative things that could work against him or could happen, he is likely to set himself up to fail and, in turn, then see such a failure as confirmation of his original thoughts. However, if he focuses on the positive and what he can bring to the course that others cannot, then he is more likely to present himself positively and feel far less stressed, if at all. One set of thoughts is likely to encourage him to feel good about himself, and, therefore, is more likely to encourage him to think in a more measured and less heated manner, while the other sets him up to experience a more difficult time.

Judgements are made based on the way we think about situations, and there has been a considerable amount of research into the types of thinking styles that are helpful and those that are not.

Types of negative thinking

There are many types of negative thoughts. You may find that you relate to some more than others.

All or nothing thinking

You see things in extreme terms such as good or bad, right or wrong, success or failure. You probably set impossible tasks and then feel bad when you do not achieve them. You may even not start tasks because you feel you cannot complete them to the desired standard.

For example:

- you planned to cook a special meal for some of your friends and then forgot to defrost the meat, and you think to yourself, '*Everything is ruined*';
- you take on a new job, one that includes things you have never done before, and your boss asks you to amend a report that you have written and you find yourself thinking, '*I'm useless at this and I will never get it*'.

EXERCISE

If you decide that *all or nothing* thinking relates to you, list two situations where you can identify this type of thinking, together with the thoughts that were going through your head at the time.

    Situation   Thoughts at the time

1.

2.

Jumping to conclusions

This is rather like believing you are telepathic and can read minds. You predict a negative outcome and then encourage it to happen by telling yourself it will, and you set up what could be called a 'self-fulfilling prophecy'.

For example:

- you have worked really hard on your first assignment for college and have not found it easy. When you get your assignment back, your tutor has stated that you have done well but there were a few areas where you could improve. Instead of feeling pleased with yourself, you find yourself saying, '*I'm pretty useless at this!*';

● you have to give a presentation to your colleagues, and it seems to go well enough. However, you get some questions that you were not expecting and then find yourself thinking, '*They don't think I have done a good enough job or else they would not be asking all these questions*'.

EXERCISE

If you decide that *jumping to conclusions* relates to you, list two situations where you can identify this type of thinking, together with the thoughts that were going through your mind at the time.

Situation	Thoughts at the time
1.	
2.	

Mental filter

A mental filter is like a sieve where you filter out everything that is good and focus only on the negative things that have happened.

For example:

● your best friend is having a special birthday, and you arrange a surprise party for her. Everyone has a good time, but you overhear a conversation where someone

79

says that it was a bit noisy and you find yourself obsessing about whether you got the sound levels wrong;

- you want to learn to swim better, but have never been that confident in the water and remember a time when your friends teased you about this. Although that was a long time ago and there are many other examples of how quickly you learn, on the basis of this experience you predict that you will be useless and do not join the class.

EXERCISE

If you decide that *mental filter* relates to you, list two situations where you can identify this type of thinking, together with the thoughts that were going through your mind at the time.

    Situation   Thoughts at the time

1.

2.

Discounting the positive

You make yourself feel unhappy by discounting your achievements and the positive things you have done. When we discount the positive we take the pleasure out of life.

For example:

- you win an award for being employee of the month. However, you say to yourself, '*That was nothing, anyone could have done that*';

- you have put a lot of work into your new garden, but have not been able to do as much as you would have liked. You tell yourself, '*I've achieved nothing really, as there are still things to do*'.

EXERCISE

If you decide that *discounting the positive* relates to you, list two situations where you can identify this type of thinking, together with the thoughts that were going through your mind at the time.

     Situation   Thoughts at the time

1

2.

Emotional reasoning

You believe that what you feel is true. So, if you feel bad, you believe it is because you have done something wrong.

For example:

- you feel awkward about social events and conclude that other people look down on you;
- you make a mistake and you find yourself thinking, '*I made a mistake, I must be dumb*'.

Labelling

Do you label yourself with terms such as '*I am a failure*', '*I am useless*', and '*I am worthless*'? Every time anything goes wrong, however small, it reinforces the label you have given yourself.

EXERCISE

If you decide that *emotional reasoning* relates to you, list two situations where you can identify this type of thinking, together with the thoughts that were going through your mind at the time.

Situation   Thoughts at the time

1.

2.

For example:

- you did not get the job you applied for and feel a failure. Because you did not do well, you say to yourself, '*I am a failure*';
- you made a mistake about the time you were due to meet someone, and because you made an error, you say to yourself, '*I am stupid*'.

EXERCISE

If you decide that *labelling* relates to you, list two situations where you can identify this type of thinking, together with the thoughts that were going through your mind at the time.

Situation   Thoughts at the time

1.

2.

Personalization and blame

You take everything personally and blame yourself even when it isn't your fault.

For example:

- you have to put together a project to present to your team, and need figures from another department, members of which do not seem to be able to get them to you in time. You find yourself feeling stressed, thinking, *'People will think I have not done a good job'*.

Alternatively, you may blame other people for what goes wrong instead of thinking about your part in events. In this case, instead of thinking that you had let people down and feeling irritated and stressed with yourself, you find yourself thinking, *'You just can't trust anyone else to do anything; they will always let you down'*.

EXERCISE

If you decide that *personalization and blame* relates to you, list two situations where you can identify this type of thinking, together with the thoughts that were going through your mind at the time.

    Situation   Thoughts at the time

1.

2.

Over-generalization

You tend to be prone to making global statements about yourself, other people, and the world.

For example:

- you are struggling with a new mobile phone. You make a mistake and think, '*I'll never get this!*';
- your male colleague builds on an idea you floated, and the boss overhears a conversation and congratulates him, and although he says you had the original idea and all he did was build on it, you find yourself thinking, '*People are all the same; you cannot trust them*'.

EXERCISE

If you decide that *over-generalizing* relates to you, list two situations where you can identify this type of thinking, together with the thoughts that were going through your mind at the time.

    Situation   Thoughts at the time

1.

2.

Shoulds and musts

Your life is full of things you think you *should be* and *must do*. You use these statements as a way of trying to motivate yourself. However, the more you tell yourself these things, the less likely you are to do them. In addition, you also end up feeling bad about yourself. Some people use 'shoulds' and 'musts' as a way of thinking about other people in a punishing way. For example, '*He should have known*', '*She must do what I want*'. When we use this type of thinking in relation to others, we are really saying we know what is right.

For example:

- you spend time believing, '*I should not be so forgetful*'; '*I must do better and how stupid of me*';
- you are having a particularly difficult time and you start thinking, '*I should be able to deal with this*'.

EXERCISE

If you decide that *shoulds and musts* relates to you, list two situations where you can identify this type of thinking, together with the thoughts that were going through your mind at the time.

    Situation   Thoughts at the time

1.

2.

Catastrophizing

When we use this type of thinking, it is rather like making a mountain out of a molehill – if there is a way of making things as bad as possible, we think it. People using this type of thinking often use lots of emotional words that predict the most awful consequences.

For example:

- your girlfriend says she wants to talk to you, and you spend the evening thinking about what she might want to say and psyching yourself up for a confrontation because you believe the discussion will be negative;

- you find that your partner has moved your CD collection and they are not in alphabetical order, as they were. He moved them so that he could clean, and you believe that he did not put them back in alphabetical order on purpose and that it is a big deal.

EXERCISE

If you decide that *catastrophizing* relates to you, list two situations where you can identify this type of thinking, together with the thoughts that were going through your mind at the time.

    Situation   Thoughts at the time

1.

2.

Stress-free thinking means learning how to challenge and change your negative thinking. Try to imagine that every time you engage in negative thinking it is like going to your building society, taking out a handful of money, and then giving it away without thought. Your emotional energy is just as valuable. It is when you face a crisis that you need to be able to call upon your reserves. After all, it is when the roof needs replacing that you are glad you have saved some money, and the same principle applies when you face an emotional crisis.

Edit your thoughts

Writing things down means you are more likely to stick to your plans. Use your journal or notebook to track your progress. If you keep all your information in one place, it means you have an independent record of your success. Everyone has bad days, and progress hardly ever goes in a straight line upwards. There are usually some setbacks along the way.

Your first step is to learn *how to* challenge your thoughts. Using the list you made of your negative thinking under the 'self-defeating thinking' heading, complete the 'faulty thinking' form below to help you identify the type of unhelpful thinking in which you are engaging. An example of a completed form is given on p. 88.

Faulty thinking form				
Situation	Self-defeating thinking	Feelings and actions	Healthy response	New approach
A	B	C	D	E

Completed example				
Situation A	Self-defeating thinking B	Feelings and actions C	Healthy response D	New approach E
You realize you have been given far too much work to clear and cannot do it by many of the deadlines that have been set by your boss.	*I can't do this and I should be able to. My boss will think I am incompetent.* **Empirical:** *Where is my evidence that my boss expects me to do it all? When I have spoken to him in the past, he has always been helpful. Maybe I should explain situation and ask for some help.* **Logical:** *Just because I have a set of deadlines, how does it logically follow that I have to keep to them?* **Pragmatic:** *Does holding on to this idea make my life better or worse?*	Anxious and stressed	*Breathing exercises to calm me down and challenge my thoughts.* **Empirical:** *There is no evidence that my boss believes I should do it all.* **Logical:** *As there is no way I can complete all these projects by the set date, it is not logical for me to keep trying but more logical for me to take action and seek guidance.* **Pragmatic:** *Even if there is an expecttion of me to complete these projects by the due date, it is not going to happen, so the ooner I sort something out the better.*	It is obvious I cannot meet the deadlines and worry about it won't change anything. I will talk to my boss and the sooner we set a realistic schedule the better as this will manage other people's expectations.

The SPACE model

Psychologist Nick Edgerton developed a different way to capture thoughts, feelings, and behaviours, which he names the SPACE model. Some people prefer this model, as they find the acronym SPACE easier to remember. What is important, regardless of whichever model you decide to use, is that you write down your thoughts as often as possible, as it is then and only then that you will be able to keep track of what you are thinking and challenge your thoughts.

S = Social context (e.g., *the situation you find yourself in*);
P = Physiology (e.g., *the sensations you experience in your body*);
A = Actions (e.g., *the behaviours and actions you engage in*);
C = Cognitions (e.g., *the thoughts you have*);
E = Emotions (e.g., *the feelings you experience*).

The A–E Model

Another way you can start to challenge your thoughts is the A–E Model, taken from Positive Psychology, devised by Martin Seligman. Given that your thoughts provide the fuel for your feelings, the A–E Model helps you control your thoughts, turning them from pessimistic and self-defeating to self-enhancing. There is no point thinking the worst when you have no evidence that it will happen, or making yourself feel bad for no good reason.

A for Adversity

Everyone faces difficult situations, and this stage sees you defining what the situation is. Think about the situation, who is involved, and be as concrete as you can in describing the event in question.

B for Beliefs

What thoughts are going around in your head? Don't censor your thoughts, just write down everything you think about the situation.

C for Consequences

How do your thoughts affect you; what do they make you feel and do?

D for Dispute

Look for some evidence to counter what you are thinking. Ask yourself what other explanation there could be. If there is more than one possibility, why believe the worst?

E for Energy

When you start to think about something differently, register how this changes the way you feel and how, in turn, this generates a series of different outcomes (see the example of a completed A–E form on p. 91).

Challenge your thoughts

Jumping to conclusions

Look for *EVIDENCE* to challenge your thinking. If you believe you *always get things wrong*, think about occasions

Completed A–E Form

A–E	Taking stock
Adversity	*I did not get the job I wanted.*
Beliefs	*I'll never get a job, I must be pretty useless!*
Consequences	*I feel awful and don't want to do any of the work I should be doing.*
	I just want to go home.
Dispute	*I've been pretty successful before, so maybe I am not useless. Maybe I was just not right for this position and they did say to keep in touch and would not have said that if I had been awful.*
Energy	*When I started to think about alternative reasons I felt so much better. Why make myself feel bad. Perhaps I need to think about the interview and what I learnt from it and apply that to the next one.*

when you *got things right*. Check out your thinking by asking people what they really think, rather than simply acting on what you believe – your beliefs are only assumptions.

Over-generalization

Learn to be your own best friend. Ask yourself what you would say to a friend in the same position. Don't you think it is strange that we are often kinder to others than we are to ourselves?

Shoulds and musts

Use the idea of 'preference' *vs.* 'absolutist' statements such as 'should'. When you use 'should', you are really saying that the world and the people in it (including yourself) absolutely must behave a certain way. For example, '*I really would prefer to get things right all the time*' instead of '*I must not get things wrong*'. There is nothing wrong with wanting to do well or wanting others to do the things we would want. However, there is *no rule* that says other people should do what we want, or that just because we want something we should have it!

All or nothing

When you find yourself thinking in an extreme way, look for the middle route. For example, could you break the task down into stages? Did you manage to do some of what you set out to do? If so, give yourself credit for what you *have* done.

Mental filter

Challenge your filter by writing down three good things that have happened each day. Watch out and listen for positive comments, and when you find yourself worrying about something someone has said, ask yourself if you are ignoring the positive comments.

Discounting the positive

When you tell yourself that what you have done does not count, stop and give yourself a pat on the back. Make a point of finding someone to speak to out loud about what you have done. For example, '*I do find it difficult to ask for help. However, I am getting better at it*'.

Emotional reasoning/labelling

When you call yourself a negative name, such as stupid, a failure, or a no-good, ask yourself what you *really* mean.

After all, what makes someone a failure? You can fail an exam, but failing at something is not a failure. It does not discount the positive.

The 'Big I, little I' exercise shown in Figure 5 can be useful. Draw the outline of a large I. This Big I represents you – then fill in the I with lots of little i's, and these i's represent different parts of your personality. For example, 'I am kind', 'I can cook', and 'I have a good sense of humour'.

Personalization and blame

When you find yourself blaming yourself (or other people) because you believe it is your entire fault, draw a

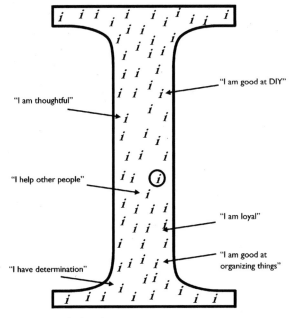

"I am thoughtful"

"I am good at DIY"

"I help other people"

"I am loyal"

"I have determination"

"I am good at organizing things"

Figure 5. Big I, little I diagram

'responsibility pie'. Think about all the factors of the situation and how many people or circumstances have contributed to the outcome. As you carve up the pie, you will see that you are only one part of a much bigger system. Only take responsibility for what is yours, learn from the situation for next time, and speak to others about their part.

When you have worked out what actions belong to whom, taking responsibility for what is yours and giving back the responsibility that belongs to other people becomes easier. Allocate a percentage of responsibility to each of the people and/or areas you have identified.

Below are some useful questions that you can ask yourself.

WHAT'S THE SITUATION?

'I feel stressed because I have offered to arrange the football club outing and it is proving really difficult to find a date that everyone can do. Most people can do the 10th, but some people are coming back to me and complaining that they cannot make that date. The venue could only offer certain dates, so we had to work within these.'

WHAT DID YOU TRY TO DO?

'I emailed everyone, set out dates, and asked for suggestions.'

WHAT PART DO YOU THINK YOU PLAYED IN THE SITUATION?

'I could have started maybe a month earlier, so diaries were not so full.'

Me = thirty per cent

WHAT PART DO OTHER PEOPLE OR CIRCUMSTANCES PLAY?

'People did take ages to respond and I had to send out more than one email.'

Club members = thirty per cent

WHAT PART DID THE VENUE PLAY?

'The venue could only offer certain dates.'

Venue: forty per cent

Catastrophizing

Notice the emotive language you are using and tone it down. Remember that things are not awful, a disaster, or a

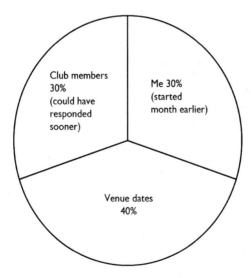

Figure 6. Ressponsibility pie chart

nightmare. This does not mean that the situation is not difficult, hard, or painful. Use words that put the situation into perspective. Ask yourself, '*What's the worst that can really happen?*'

Life rules

Some people hold negative beliefs about themselves. For example, you may believe you are a failure, worthless, a bad person, stupid, unlovable, or unattractive. These beliefs shape your actions in everyday life. These beliefs can be seen as the rules that dictate the way we manage our daily lives.

An example of a life rule would be if you thought you were unlovable and then spent your life avoiding or sabotaging your personal relationships as a way of avoiding facing what you felt was your inability to be loved. You may live your life believing that '*I am not a good person and no one will love me*', and when people begin to get close to you, you would rather push them away than to have this view of yourself confirmed. '*I've met a really nice man, but there is no point in taking it further as he will find out that I am not worthy of love and therefore it will all end anyway.*'

People whose life rules are about over-achieving as a way of fending off beliefs about failure, being unworthy, or not being lovable tend to feel good only when they feel safe, and this usually means that, although unhappy with being on their own, it feels less threatening when they are. If you believe yourself to be lacking in some way, you may believe that you are a worthless person because you do not conform to whatever you believe the standard to be. This also means that when things go wrong, which they invariably will do, you may find yourself feeling fearful.

A person who believes she is only safe from her beliefs about being unlovable if she remains alone may find herself feeling very frightened if she is faced with a situation where she needs to prove herself in some way. Some people believe they are bad people, and that if people really knew them, rather than the mask they present to the world, they would be disliked and seen as a fraud. It is helpful to identify your basic beliefs so that you can use the counter-measures described in this book to change the ways you perceive yourself.

Beliefs about yourself, others, and the world have been formed by the messages you received from:

- family;
- friends;
- the world.

Over time you have been conditioned to think in a certain way, and it takes time to change your belief, regardless of how motivated you are to do so.

Demands that may increase your stress

There are three types of demands we make of ourselves in the form of 'musts', and these are:

Demands about self, e.g., '*I must always get it right*' (creates stress, anxiety, shame, and guilt).
Demands about others, e.g., '*You must behave well otherwise it is awful*' (creates irritability, frustration, and anger).

Demands about the world, e.g., '*the world should be a fair and just place*' (creates self pity, addictive behaviour, and depression).

To help you identify your personal musts and the types of beliefs your musts are based on, write yourself an '*I must, otherwise I am*' list, as follows.

Demands of self

I must . . ., otherwise . . .
e.g., *I must be strong and capable, otherwise I am a failure.*

Demands of others

You must . . ., otherwise . . .
e.g., *You must agree with me, otherwise I am wrong and that would be awful.*

Demands of the world

The world must . . ., otherwise . . .
e.g., *The world must treat me well if I work hard and do my best, otherwise it is not fair.*

When you have identified the personal demands you make of yourself, others, and the world, you need to set about challenging them. Do this in the same way you identified your automatic negative thoughts earlier.

Challenging your demands

You can challenge the demands you are making of yourself in the following ways:

- consider the impact your demand has on you and those around you;
- identify how you know when the demand is activated (i.e., the thoughts, feelings, and behaviours you experience).
- think about how the demand came about and the life experiences that sustain it;
- consider the advantages and disadvantages of holding on to your demand;
- identify a more appropriate way of rephrasing your demand, which fits with life as it is now;
- think about how you are going to put your new demand into action.

What if I can't identify a demand but suspect there is one?

Sometimes you find yourself saying things like, '*It would be awful*', or '*that's just not right*'. When you make statements like these, it doesn't seem at first sight as if there is a core belief in operation. You could find a situation triggers a strong feeling and, although you identify your negative automatic thought and challenge it, you still seem to feel unhappy.

If this is the case, ask yourself a series of questions and, rather like an archaeological dig, these will help you uncover your core belief. It is sometimes helpful to see your thought at the beginning of a long chain and your core beliefs at the other end. You have to identify each link in the chain and, as you do so, you get nearer the end of the chain that holds your core belief.

For example:

Situation: You are asked to manage a group of people and have never been in a supervisory capacity before.

Feeling: Anxiety

Thought: I can't do this, I'll really mess it up.

1. Ask yourself: '*What is so awful about not having managed before?*'
   Answer: '*It means I will get it wrong and do a bad job.*'

2. Ask yourself: '*Supposing that were true, what would that mean?*'
   Answer: '*It would mean people would think badly of me.*'

3. Ask yourself: 'And if they did, what would that mean?'
   Answer: '*People would laugh at me.*'

4. Ask yourself: '*And if they did?*'
   Answer: '*That would be awful.*'

5. Ask yourself: 'What would be awful?'
   Answer: '*They would think I was not capable.*'

6. Ask yourself: '*Suppose they did think you weren't capable?*'
   Answer: '*They would know how stupid I am.*'

7. Ask yourself: '*So what does being seen as stupid mean to me?*'
   Answer: '*I must never be seen as stupid otherwise this means I am a failure.*'

You end up with a core belief, which, in this case, is 'I can't take risks because if it goes wrong I will be seen as stupid and this will mean I am a failure'.

Summary

One way of looking at the role self-defeating thinking plays in shaping your life is to consider the three-stage relationship between automatic thoughts, demands/life rules, and core beliefs. Core beliefs are the conclusions you draw about yourself as a person, as in thinking you are fundamentally bad, worthless, or a failure.

Automatic thoughts are triggered by the situations you find yourself in: for example, being asked to do something you do not want to do, and thinking, *'I can't do this'*. Another way of thinking about demands is to see them as 'if . . . then' rules: for example, *'if I try something new in tackling a project, then I might fail and that would be awful'*. Core beliefs are absolutist beliefs we hold about ourselves such as, *'I am useless'*.

A simple way of thinking of this three-stage model is outlined in Figure 7.

Putting it all together: a model for understanding your stress

Figure 7 provides you with a model for understanding and analysing your stress.

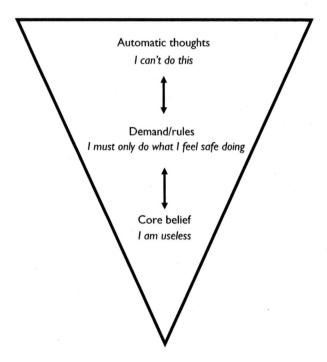

Figure 7.   A model for understanding and analysing your stress

The concept of good and bad moods

Having completed the exercises above, you will probably begin to see that you can change the way you think about situations, and by doing this you can change your feelings, and your actions will, as a consequence, also be different.

The 'mood' we are in also very often has an impact on how we behave. For example, if I am tired I am likely to be affected by situations more negatively than if I am rested and well. If things are not going so well for me on a personal level, this also may influence how I react and I may be more cautious than I normally would be. You could say that the 'mood' I am in will either help or hinder me in the way I deal with situations. However, I also have choices about how I can shape my own moods by choosing to think about what I am thinking and why, and to change the way I feel by changing the way I think. As we saw earlier, all kinds of things can affect our mood – sleep, stress, alcohol, etc. Therefore, if it is possible for you to be in a 'good mood' one day and let things wash over you, then it is possible for you to re-create that mood, or at least modify your 'bad mood' so that it does not damage you or anyone else.

Table 5 is an example of a mood table, and is followed by an exercise in which you can create one for yourself and examine your positive and negative thinking with regard to three different situations.

Table 5. Mood table

Situation	Good mood I think . . .	Bad mood I think . . .
Bus comes late.	*Well, at least it is a nice day, and I can enjoy the sunshine.*	*Typical – never a bus when you want one.*
Two cats playing on a wall.	*How funny cats can be and they do look cute.*	*Why can't people control their pets? Bet they are pooping in other people's gardens.*
Friend not answering his mobile phone.	*Wonder what he is up to then. Will catch him later.*	*I really wanted to speak to him. No one is ever available when I want to speak to them.*

EXERCISE

1. Think of three situations that you find yourself in where, depending on your mood, you may see things completely differently, and complete the mood table below.

Mood table

Situation	Good mood I think . . .	Bad mood I think . . .

(continued)

2. Now that you have identified the three situations, look at what you have written down in
relation to your 'bad mood' and identify which
types of faulty thinking you engage in when you
think this way. Once you have done this, look at
your 'good mood' and identify what type of
thinking makes you respond in a more positive
way.

When you have completed the exercise you will see more
clearly how good moods and bad moods are based on what
we are thinking at the time. If you see thinking as a kind of
self-talk then if you can talk yourself into a bad mood you
can talk yourself out! Our mood affects our stress levels, so
the better the mood the better the stress levels.

Learn to accept yourself

The tips on the pages that follow are based on the princi-
ples of a therapy called Rational Emotive Behaviour
Therapy, or REBT for short. You need to learn to like yourself, and to do this you need to accept yourself. They offer
practical suggestions and ways to begin the process of self-
acceptance. Self-acceptance is the arduous process of learning to like yourself 'warts and all'. Self-acceptance helps you
to decrease your stress and increase your confidence.

Tips to help you like yourself

- Remember that human beings are not perfect and
  that *includes you*! There is no such thing as a person

who is 100% right, good, capable, or strong. If you spend your life believing that perfection exists you will always be disappointed, unhappy, stressed, and in danger of being anxious and depressed. There is nothing wrong with wanting to do things well, to be a good worker, student, parent, partner, or friend. Set yourself realistically high but not impossibly perfectionist standards.

- Remember that everyone is equal, regardless of ability. It is possible for someone to have greater talents or skills than you without being a *better person*. Stop comparing yourself to other people, as this can only lead to feelings of anxiety, resentment, or disappointment. If you admire someone for something they have done, there is nothing wrong with thinking about the quality they possess or the way they did something, trying to identify the key components so you can model your behaviour on theirs and learn from what they have done. Modelling yourself is not the same as comparing yourself. There may be differences in what people can do, but there is no difference in the basic worth of each human being. One person is not 'better' than another.

- There is no such thing as a 'global rating' on human goodness or badness. No one is ever *all good* or *all bad*. Good people sometimes do bad things and bad people sometimes do good things. If you behave in a way that you think better about, then take the appropriate action. For example: apologise, explain, and see what you can do to put things right. However, doing something you later regret does not make you a bad person, just as doing one good deed does not make someone a saint. If you keep on seeing yourself and/or others in this all or nothing way, you place unrealistic pressure on yourself and on others.

- Over-generalization (see p. 91) is where you exaggerate one aspect of your behaviour (e.g., *'Because I did not get that interview it means I never will'*). If you want to conquer your stress, it is important that you do not judge the *whole* of you on just one *part* of your behaviour; for example, *'I may not have got that job but I learnt a lot from the interview and that will help me in the future'*. Keep things in proportion. Blowing things out of proportion wastes time and energy. Confident people deal with situations. The more confident you are, the less stressed you are likely to be.
- Remember to work on dropping the *shoulds* and *musts,* as all they do is lead you to develop a conditional outlook on yourself. Dropping *shoulds, musts,* and *have tos* does not mean abdicating your responsibilities – it simply means stopping putting yourself down.
- Remember that self-acceptance is hard work. It requires energy and commitment and consistent work to make it happen.

You also need to:

- Learn to respect yourself – you are as valuable as everyone else.
- Live a lifestyle that is supportive of your health – there is no point making yourself ill from overwork or abusing your body. Why be stressed when you know that stress causes harm to you? If you do this, you are likely to increase your stress. For example, caffeine products are likely to increase your susceptibility to

stress. Caffeine is a stimulant and, as people who are stressed (as we saw earlier under the stress response section) produce stress hormones, stimulants such as caffeine help increase the production of these hormones.

- Engage in supportive relationships and carry out the life audit that follows. Work at your relationships, make sure you have a variety and cultivate them as you would your garden plants. Tending to friendships pays you back tenfold with the love and concern others will feel and show towards you.

- Set goals for yourself specifically designed to improve your life and diminish your stress. When you undertake your annual life audit, set yourself a series of goals for the year. Decide what you want to change and how you will do it. The changes that you make and what you learn about yourself all go towards your developing new life skills and increasing your confidence and sense of well-being while decreasing your stress.

- Recognize that change cannot be achieved overnight and that you will need to keep on working at challenging negative attitudes about yourself. I know this has been said more than once, but that's because it is so important. Negative thoughts bring negative reactions and more stress into daily living.

- Spend time and money on yourself – you are worth it! Learn to pamper yourself. Many people's stress is increased because of the way the individual drives him or herself; therefore, taking time out and enjoying life is a way of countering this tendency.

- Remember that you need to take responsibility for your own life. It is all too easy to blame other people or 'bad luck' for situations. However bad your situation, you *do* have choices. Sometimes you have to give yourself what I call a 'therapeutic kick up the backside'. When things go wrong, it is helpful to allow yourself to feel your feelings, to express your emotions appropriately, and to seek support from others. It is not helpful to spend time raging about how things should be, as this will not change the situation and is likely to make it worse rather than better.

Ask yourself if there is a payoff for continuing to engage in a particular behaviour. For example, if you allow others to make all the decisions for you, the payoff may be that you never have to face 'being in the wrong', and you can always blame them for the way things have turned out. However, behaving this way is more likely to increase your stress levels rather than decrease them. The more control people take, the less stressed they often feel.

Learn to appreciate yourself

If you have been stressed and lacking in confidence for a long time, you may find it hard to identify and appreciate your good points. Go back to p. 93 and complete the Big I, Little I exercise, if you have not done so already. If you need more help, ask yourself the following questions.

- What am I able to do?
- What do I like about myself?
- What have I learnt in life?
- How would someone else describe me?
- How will I ensure I actually practise these skills – what might get in the way?

Gladeana McMahon

The life audit

The life audit is a technique to help you to identify the areas of your life you would benefit from changing. A life audit should be undertaken on an annual basis, with quarterly 'check-ups' to monitor progress.

A life audit is a way of working out what in life you are happy with, need to get more of, or need to stop doing. Once you have completed the audit itself, the next step is to set about making changes to those areas of your life you have identified as needing attention. There is no point in working out what you like or dislike unless you are prepared to change the things you are unhappy about and increase the things you like. People who suffer from stress very often just let life happen – although they may scream, shout, feel anxious, cry, or get depressed, they may not do anything productive to change their situation. The life audit is one way for you to take up that control.

EXERCISE

Write down all the things you like and dislike about each of the following eight areas of your life:

- Living environment (e.g., *flat, house, geographical area*)
- Family (e.g., *family of origin, children*)
- Personal relationship(s) (e.g., *partner*)
- Friends/social life (e.g., *friendships, hobbies, outings*)
- Work/career (e.g., *current job, future aspirations*)
- Finances (e.g., *budgeting, savings, pensions, investments*)
- Health (e.g., *diet, exercise, stress management*)
- Inner soul/spirit (e.g., *your sense of purpose in life*)

Example – life audit

Finances

Like	Dislike
Having a good budgeting system	*I need to sort out my pension*
Setting up a holiday fund means I now get better holidays and don't worry about the cost	*Check to see if there are cheaper utility companies*

Consider each of the things you don't like and ask yourself what you could do to change the situation. Research suggests that you are far more likely to carry out your plans if you write them down.

Action plans

Finances

Dislike	Action plan
Sort out pension	*Ask Julie for the name of her financial adviser and also check on the comparison websites to see what is out there.*
Find cheaper utility companies	*Mum said she had a great deal, so speak to her and also print off a list and see who is offering the best deal.*

Distraction

Distraction techniques are helpful when you are stressed and keep having thoughts that are making you feel uncomfortable or are undermining your efforts. Distraction is a way if taking your attention away from what is

happening and on to something else. When you find
yourself beginning to feel stressed, you need to decide not
to think about your thoughts, and then engage your mind
with something else. Have you ever found yourself in the
position of beginning to experience a sense of frustration
only to find that something happened to distract you and
your feeling changed?

There are three types of distraction:

1. Paying attention to what is going on around you – try
    guessing the ages of people in the room, or listen to
    someone else's conversation, or decide to count as
    many round objects as you can see in the room.
2. Physical activity – try cleaning, tidying up, or finding
    tasks to do.
3. Engage in some form of mental activity – recite your
    times tables, say the alphabet backwards, or do a
    crossword.

STRESS-FREE EMOTIONS

Learn to be emotionally smart

Emotional intelligence is about learning to be emotionally smart. It is not always the person with the highest IQ who does best. Emotionally smart people get the most from managing their own and other people's emotions. If you can learn the skills of emotional smartness, it will help you to overcome your stress. When you are stressed you may find that people behave differently towards you. They may decide not to consult you because they do not want to add to your burdens, or because when they do you do not listen to what they have to say or just say no because you don't want another thing to deal with. They may talk about you behind your back, and you may get a reputation as someone who is best to be avoided.

The skills fall into five key areas.

Identifying my emotions

Emotionally smart people are able to identify their own emotions. This means learning to tell other people how you feel. It means taking responsibility for your own emotions by starting sentences with '*I feel* . . .'.

Managing your emotions

Emotions can be difficult, and emotionally smart people know when to take care of themselves. For example, when you find things difficult what are the things you do to take care of yourself? Do you have a long hot bath and relax?

Do you talk to a friend? Do you get a DVD or video and watch that? There are times when you need to take care of other people's emotions and there are times when you need to motivate yourself and others.

EXERCISE

How to identify emotions

1. Look at the series of positive and negative words below. Place a tick against the words you think describe you best.
2. Why have you chosen those particular words?
3. If you were to change your negative words to positive ones, what would you have to do?

Positive	Negative
Empathic	Angry
Loving	Anxious
Happy	Jealous
Joyful	Possessive
Caring	Remorseful
Enthusiastic	Envious
Warm	Resentful

EXERCISE

Taking care of my emotions

List two ways in which you take care of yourself and two ways in which you take care of other people (e.g., warm bath, ring a friend, encourage someone to talk).

Me	Others
1.	1.
2.	2.

Other people's emotions

Emotionally smart people have developed the ability to pick up other people's emotions. Using skills such as empathy (the ability to imagine what it might feel like to see the world from another perspective), a smart person considers how the other person might be feeling, realizing that such recognition can encourage a more co-operative relationship.

EXERCISE

How do I show my understanding of others?

Think about people and situations where you feel a connection with what the person is feeling. This ability of being able to imagine what it is like for the other person is called empathy. Choose friends or use characters from films or television. Think about why you empathize with the person you have chosen.

Those I empathize with   *Reasons I empathize with them*

(continued)

Now, list all the ways in which you would demonstrate your understanding to another person (e.g.,
*giving the person my full attention or using certain
words*).

Learning to motivate yourself

There are times when strong emotions get in the way.
There may be times when it is better to put off your own
needs and wants for a future pay-off. Some people find
themselves so caught up in their immediate emotions that
they forget there is a bigger picture.

EXERCISE

When have I motivated myself or others?

Think of two situations where you have motivated
yourself or other people. In particular, think of situations where there has been strong emotion. How
did you cope with the strong emotion so that you
were able to complete the task in hand?

Situation 1

What happened?

(continued)

What I did:

Situation 2

What happened?

What I did:

Healthy relationships

Life is full of relationships, so it makes sense to consider the behaviours that help to create happy and productive relationships while recognizing those that destroy them.

EXERCISE

Ways of creating positive relationships

List three ways to cultivate a relationship (e.g., ringing people regularly, remembering special events, or listening to a friend's problems)

1.

2.

3.

Learning to appreciate yourself and others

How do you feel when I ask you to

list five things you could do better?;
list five things that have gone well and you are pleased with?

I suspect you found the first question easier to answer and the second more difficult. Most people neglect the power of praise and appreciation – the bottom line is that appreciation and praise motivate.

Some people fear that if they praise themselves or others, it will lead to a slacking off in effort or that they will be seen as weak. It is well documented that children who are constantly criticized are more likely to have poor confidence and to stop trying to improve. They may even feel more stressed because they feel they are not good enough or are failing.

Success encourages success and every time you or someone else does something well (even partially well) it is one more step towards building a stress-free life.

EXERCISE

Past praise

1. The last time I praised myself was . . .

(continued)

---

2. The last time I praised someone else was . . .

Future praise

Think of two things that you know you could praise yourself for and complete the following sentences.

I was pleased with myself when I

I thought I did well to

Other people's emotions

If you have the ability to read and understand other people's emotions, you have a great advantage in influencing people's attitudes towards you.

Reading emotions means:

1. *Watching body language*

   People's body language and voice tone tell you a lot about how they are feeling and your body language is also a way of communicating. Angry people often try to overpower others – they stare at people, raise their voices, and look menacing, sometimes invading another person's space.

119

EXERCISE

My epitaph

Use the following space to write your own epitaph. How would you like to be remembered? I've written mine so that you can see what one could look like.

She lived her life to the full and always tried to treat others as she would like to be treated.

Write yours here.

When you wrote your epitaph, what feelings came up for you? Look at what you have written and consider whether you are living your life in a way that is likely to make your words come true. What changes do you need to make and how will you set about making those changes?

---

2. *Listen to the words*

    What do the words tell you? Sometimes people tell you what they are feeling (e.g., *I feel cross about what you have just said*). If you think of the words you use, what impact do you think they have? What do they say about you?

3. *Use your empathy*

    Empathy, as we explored earlier, is the ability to imagine what it might be like to see the world wearing someone else's shoes. Empathy can be expressed through statements such as '*You sound frustrated*', and '*I imagine you were very unhappy about that*'.

How to deal with strong emotion

Strong emotions can be disturbing for both the person experiencing them and for those around at the time. Many people feel uncomfortable with expressing emotions or being around people who are expressing them.

Strong emotions could include anxiety, anger, or severe emotional distress. Sometimes you may be frightened by the strength of the emotion you feel; for example, being overwhelmed with fear. Being around an angry person can be difficult as anger can often be felt by others, and this can either make the other person feel anxious or make them cut the contact short as they find it an uncomfortable emotion.

It is easier to handle strong emotions if you make a point of acknowledging them. If you suppress feelings, never admitting them to yourself or others, they get stored. Sooner or later there are simply too much stored emotion, the natural suppression mechanism stops working, and a sudden outpouring takes place.

Some people believe they should let all their emotions show all the time. These people lack emotional intelligence, as they influence other people's attitudes towards them by being overly dramatic and emotional.

There are, of course, times when strong emotions are understandable; for example, if you had just had bad news or if you needed to defend yourself against violent attack.

Exercise

When was the last time you felt a strong emotion?

Think of the last time you experienced a strong emotion – what had happened? What did you feel? How did you deal with your emotion and what was the outcome? When you have completed the exercise, look at your reactions and ask yourself whether you are happy with what you did. If you are not happy, what could you have done differently?

What actually happened:

What I felt at the time:

What I did at the time:

Outcome:

What could I have done differently?

Don't put things off!

Stress is overcome by tackling life head-on as much as you can. Make a list of all the things you have put off.

Procrastination tends to compound problems. The more you mean to do, but never get around to doing, the more stress you are likely to experience. If you have a lot of things on your list you cannot do them all at once, so why not rate them in terms of difficulty, for example by using a scale of 0–10:

0 1 2 3 4 5 6 7 8 9 10

(0 = easy and 10 = really hard)

Examples:
Learning to drive   = 3
Saying no   = 5
Making time for myself = 7

Once you have drawn up this list, start with items that have a rating of between three and seven. Anything rated more than a seven may be too difficult for you at the beginning of the process. Conversely, anything less than a three may be too easy.

Always remember to praise yourself on your achievements. Think about *what you have* managed to do rather than what you believe you *should* have been doing. Keeping this kind of a record provides you with evidence of the goals you have set and your success in dealing with them.

Everyone has bad days, days when you feel that nothing has been achieved or changed. By keeping these details in your journal you have a written record of the improvements you have made and these help you to evaluate your progress realistically.

Get moving

Apart from exercise being physically healthy, it is also good for our psychological well-being. Research suggests that even mild exercise can have a positive effect. Simply walking a couple of miles each day and walking up and down stairs can do the trick. Exercise not only relieves stress, it also releases naturally produced chemicals which can raise your mood, as well as helping you to find an outlet for pent-up emotion. A number of people who are prone to stress find that exercise has a calming effect.

Guilt

Some people who are stressed also feel guilty. We often say that we feel guilty, but guilt is not so much a feeling as a thought process. When you say you feel guilty it usually means:

- you have broken one of your value rules, e.g., '*I must always be a good person and think of others*';
- you think only about the outcome of what you believe you have done or not done, e.g., '*I was too short my with friend the other day*'.

These types of guilt are either about the *actions you have taken*, or the *choices you have made*, and the consequences of your choices. A value rule is part of the moral code by which you live your life, whereas an outcome is more about what you have done.

There are some people who believe they are guilty simply because they are alive. Someone who feels guilty, but cannot tell you why, may experience this kind of guilt. This type of guilt stays with such people throughout life unless they change the way they think about themselves and the world.

If you have made a mistake, it makes sense to put it right. Try to do something to put the situation right. If you simply feel guilty without taking action, you are likely to avoid people, places, and activities that remind you of the guilt you feel.

You can deal with guilt by

- asking yourself what you actually feel guilty about;
- asking yourself if you were to find yourself in exactly the same situation today would you behave any differently;
- thinking about the way your core beliefs influence the way you live your life and whether it is possible for anyone to live up to all of those core beliefs all of the time;
- remembering '*bad things happen to good people and good people sometimes do bad things*';
- examining your 'thinking style' for examples of the kind of self-defeating thoughts described on p. 64;
- remembering that you are a fallible human being;
- realizing that if there is something you can do to change the situation for others, then doing so;
- not hiding away from the world – it won't make things better, it will just make you feel worse;
- learning to forgive yourself and remembering that forgiveness is a choice.

Use the 'Big I, Little I' (p. 93) to remind yourself of your positive points and use the 'Responsibility Pie' (p. 94) to help you work out who is responsible for what.

125

Cost–benefit analysis

It can be hard to change your behaviour, particularly if you have been acting in a certain way for a long time. A 'cost–benefit analysis' can help you identify the costs and the benefits of behaving in a certain way.

Use the cost–benefit sheet below to work out what is happening. You can write down all the benefits of continuing to act the way you are on the right-hand side of the page. Then on the left-hand side of the page you write down all the costs (emotional and practical) of continuing as you are.

Once you have completed both columns of the form, you will be in a better position to make decisions about what you want to do. If you want to change you need to decide what you need to do.

Cost–benefit analysis model
Name: Mary Stressful   Date: 10/10/10
Situation: *I have to do all that I am asked to do*

COST	BENEFIT
• Feel overwhelmed • I never have time for me • I can never feel I have achieved all I want to • I feel anxious and stressed most of the time	• *Err . . . can't find one*

The role of assertiveness

Assertiveness means asking for what you want and saying what you feel, while respecting the needs and rights of others. Many people think that being assertive is rather like being in the SAS – you take no prisoners. This is not the case. Anyone who thinks this has aggression mixed up with assertion. Some people also think that assertiveness training is only useful to people who are passive and anxious. However, this is very far from the truth, as assertiveness training is also of tremendous value to people who experience anger as their primary way of dealing with situations. What assertion training does is to provide you with the tools and strategies that you need to be able to deal with situations calmly, thoughtfully, and in a way that gives you the best chance of getting what you want out of a situation in the best possible way. The more you can do this, the less stress you will experience.

The more assertive you become the more you realize that 'compromise' is not a dirty word and that people who compromise get more of what they want from the world around them. People who are stressed often see every situation as one of either 'win or lose', and yet most of life is about finding a middle way.

Truly assertive people look for what is called a 'win–win' situation and take responsibility for their own actions. Becoming more assertive improves the way we can communicate with others. Most colleges and evening institutes are likely to offer short courses on assertiveness. There is more about assertion in the next section – Stress-Free Actions.

Shame and humiliation

You can feel shame because you believe you have broken one of your value rules – one you hold about yourself or one you believe about others. If you believe you have behaved in a way frowned on by friends, family, or society, you may feel shame. You may remember the term catastrophizing from the Stress-Free Thinking section of this book. You tell yourself that it is 'awful' you feel a certain thing or have behaved in a certain way. 'Awfulizing' is often expressed in terms of criticism about personal weakness . . . '*If people thought I was being selfish then that would be awful.*'

People who experience shame have a great capacity for avoiding people and places that remind them of what they see as their weakness.

Humiliation usually means you believe you have lost status in some way. Humiliation is closely linked to the same kind of thought processes linked to shame and guilt, in particular around the issue of worrying about how others will somehow think less of you as a result of your loss of status.

How to deal with shame and humiliation

You can ask yourself the following.

- Do I really believe someone thinks less of me as a result of what I have done and, if so, why? (Remember to use the skills you have learnt in the 'Stress-Free Thinking' section of this book.
- Would I think less of someone who had gone through an identical experience?

If you have answered 'no' to both questions, why hold yourself responsible when you would not treat others the same way?

Dealing with worry

Stressed people worry just as much as, and sometimes more than, other people. So many people worry about every aspect of life. Things go wrong and there will be times when you are worried. For example, if your mother was diagnosed with breast cancer, it would be normal for you to be concerned. The whole area of fear can be rated in terms of mild, moderate, or severe feelings. Mild fear could be seen as worry, whereas severe fear could be seen as absolute terror. Stress can also be rated as mild, moderate, and severe, and an individual's reactions to each of these stages could range from being mildly stressed, to moderately stressed, to extremely stressed.

How to worry constructively

Think about the following:

- 39% of the things you worry about never happen;
- 32% of things you worry about have already happened;
- 21% of your worries are over trivialities;
- 9% of your worries relate to important issues where you have legitimate cause for concern.

(Note: a total of 101%, due to rounding up.)

If we stopped worrying this would not be helpful, as a certain amount of concern can help you think through what you could do and provides you with the opportunity of being cautious so that you can explore all the options to come up with the best course of action.

129

Your worry notebook

Take any notebook and divide it into four sections, using the headings shown in the example below.

WORRIES FOR TODAY	
Events that might happen	Today's events

1. Things of concern that might happen	**3. Insignificant things**
I have to pick up my daughter but also get the dry cleaning, and I am expecting a parcel and what if the parcel comes while I am out?	*I keep meaning to replace that plate that I broke which goes with the dinner service and I keep forgetting and it worries me.*
2. Things that have happened	**4. Important things**
I forgot to pay mum back the £5 I borrowed and only got it back to her much later than I said I would.	*They have cut our hours at work and the mortgage has gone up and I am not sure how we will manage.*

Make the entries for headings 1, 2 and 3 before you go to bed. Choose the time of day you are at your strongest and brightest to complete section 4.

When it comes to section 4, you need to remember that *Worrying about a problem does not solve it – doing something about it does.* If you do not make a decision to do something positive you can end up making a decision by default. No action still has an outcome. You need to decide whether you want to be in control (as much as is possible), or if you are going to just let things happen. There is *always* a choice.

Half an hour a day

Set aside half an hour a day and label this your 'worry time'; during this time, feel free to worry about anything you like. It is best if you allocate the same time of day each day and avoid undertaking this exercise late in the evening. When you find yourself worrying outside of your 'worry time', take a deep breath and put off your thoughts until your allocated time.

Many people find that this exercise helps them deal with worry in a way that contains it and stops it from taking over.

Relaxation

When you feel stressed it is useful to do some of the relaxation exercises mentioned earlier. There are many forms of relaxation, as we discussed, and some require physical movement while others require nothing more than breathing or visualization techniques.

How to use coping imagery to deal with negative emotions

According to research, when you visualize a positive outcome you are more likely to get one. Coping imagery is used as a way of preparing yourself for events.

Maximum benefit is gained from the above technique when you practise it frequently.

If you find it hard to use your imagination, try the following exercise to improve your visualization skills and

EXERCISE

If you do not have a current or future situation that causes you concern, think about the last one that did.

- First, write out a 'problem list' of all the people, places, and situations you feel uncomfortable with or in. Use the 0–10 scale as a way of rating the degree of discomfort you feel (0 = no discomfort and 10 = maximum discomfort).
- Once you have made out your list, choose something that has a rating of no more than seven. (Choosing a higher rating would make it too difficult and choosing a lower rating would not be challenging enough.) After all, you want to succeed, and if you make your task too difficult you may set yourself up to fail.
- Now, close your eyes and imagine yourself at the beginning of your task. Use all your senses to imagine the sights, the sounds, and the smells. Think about what you would say and what you would do. Think about what you think the other person(s) might say. Use coping strategies like breathing, anchoring, and helpful self-talk to help you deal with the event.
- Now practise this visualization two or three times, each time seeing yourself coping with the situation. You may find that practising this exercise actually reduces your original rating, even though you are using only your imagination. It is as if your brain is fooled into believing that you really *have done* whatever you set out to do. Once you have practised this exercise a few times the next task is actually to do it!

develop your imagination 'muscles'. Like everything else in life, with practice, your ability will improve.

- Imagine looking at the sky at night.
- Choose one star and watch it become brighter and then dimmer. Do this repeatedly.
- See if you can track the star across the sky.

STRESS-FREE ACTIONS

Graded exposure

If you want to overcome your stress, you have to challenge your behaviour. Stress makes us behave in ways that are not helpful, and when you give in to your feelings all you do is give power to them and you may well find that these feelings increase. If this is the case, the likelihood of positive outcomes becomes less feasible. For example, you are on the phone to arrange for someone to come to service your cable TV and are passed from one person to another; you are feeling increasingly stressed and frustrated. You find you are raising your voice and pacing around the room.

If you really want to conquer your stress, you need to engage in what is called graded exposure. Graded exposure means that you start to face those situations you find difficult, engaging in a range of coping strategies to help you deal with your feelings. Research has shown that when you face a difficult situation your feelings will peak, and if you can stay in the situation after that, your feelings will come down to a more bearable level.

There are four stages to using graded exposure.

Stage one

Make a list of all the situations you find difficult to deal with without getting stressed. Then, using a scale of 0–8 (0 = no stress; 8 = extreme stress), rate each of the items on the list.

134

Stage two

Now that you have rated the items, place them in order of degree of difficulty.

Stage three

You may want to select the easiest item on your list as the first one to start with. One word of advice here though – it is probably best to start with an item you have rated at four. If you try to deal with anything more than a four, it may be too difficult for you to manage. If you start with an item rated less than four, it may be too easy. An item rated four is hard enough for you to get the benefit of the exercise in terms of stretching yourself, but not so high that it is asking too much of you.

Stage four

Plan how you will tackle your task and what coping strategies you will use; for example, breathing, having a coping statement that you will repeat to yourself, or using distraction. Repeat this activity as many times as it takes for you to manage it without difficulty.

When you have successfully dealt with this item, go back to your list and move on to the next item.

The trick with graded exposure is that you must undertake the tasks regularly and for prolonged periods of time, so that the stress passes and you become more proficient at using your coping strategies.

Sometimes progress may seem slow and you may want to give up. However, progress is progress and giving up will only make matters worse, as by doing so you will convince yourself that you will never change. One small step at a time is still a step in the right direction. Do not discount what you have achieved. Learning to recognize your achievements, however small you think they are, is a way of increasing your confidence. When you find yourself 'discounting the positives', using statements such as, '*It's ridiculous, what a small thing I did today*', say to yourself, '*I managed to handle that situation better than I would have normally, and with much less stress*'.

Using coping imagery to reduce stress

Dealing with stress is not easy, and you will need a range of coping strategies, from changing the way you think about situations to calming your body down by breathing. In addition, you can use imagery as a way of helping yourself to manage your feelings and the situations you may face.

An imagery technique helps to prepare you for the event as a way to help decrease your stress and practise the type of coping strategies that might be helpful. When stress levels have fallen to four or five, using your rating scale, it might be the time to consider tackling the task you have set yourself.

Coping imagery requires a person to imagine him or herself coping in a situation that usually causes them to become stressed. The following describes the sequence of action for dealing with a specific situation, say dealing with the daily school run and getting to the office on time, where you tend to react negatively and with increasing stress levels when you find yourself held up.

1. First, write out a 'fears list', outlining a hierarchy of difficult situations associated with this situation using a scale of 0–8.
   Consider Francesca's list as an example.
   Thinking about getting the children into the car on time   =3
   Driving to the school when the traffic is heavy =4
   Dealing with the traffic from the school to the office =5
   Arriving at the office late   =8

2. Once you have your own list made out, choose something that has a rating of no more than four or five. (Choosing anything with a higher rating would make it too difficult. A rating lower than two would probably not be challenging enough.)

   Francesca decided to take dealing with heavy traffic while driving to the school as this was rated four. She then went on to imagine the following.

3. Close your eyes and imagine yourself sitting in the car with the children talking in the back. Use all your senses to imagine the sights (traffic, pedestrians) and smells (the newly cleaned upholstery). Imagine yourself watching the traffic in front of you moving very slowly. Using coping strategies like breathing, anchoring, and helpful self-talk, imagine yourself dealing with these feelings in a helpful manner.

   (Francesca had already been taught how to relax through breathing, and had anchored a pleasant memory to the wedding ring she always wore. She knew how her body

137

> *responded when stressed, in releasing stress hormones into the system, and that apart from feeling stressed, she also felt anxious about being late. She had put together some helpful self-talk such as 'I can't do anything about the traffic and being late is not the end of the world; it is better I stay calm'.)*

4. If you are using your coping strategies, your stress is likely to abate, and once it has reduced to, say a three, you can choose something a little more difficult from the list you have drawn up.

Francesca practised this exercise for two days, three times a day, until her feelings of stress had subsided to a one. Monday was usually a particularly bad day for traffic, so she decided to repeat this exercise twice on Sunday evening, together with her breathing exercises. She told herself that her objective was to stay calmer and get to the school feeling more relaxed.

She found that the exercise went well, and although her stress went up to a five when sitting in the car for real, it took very little time for it to subside. She used all her coping strategies and was very pleased with what she achieved. Her success gave her the confidence to increase the degree of difficulty, using the items on her list.

To gain the maximum benefit from the above technique, you need to practise it frequently. Once you feel confident enough, you need to follow through with a real life event. When you undertake a live exercise, you should use all the coping strategies you have practised in your imagination. It is also important to remember to break down your exercises into small, manageable steps. Trying to do too much will put too much strain on you and could lead to a sense of failure and feelings of stress. Remember that old maxim '*success breeds success*'.

If you find it hard to use your imagination, try the following exercise to improve your visualization skills and develop your imagination 'muscles'. Like everything else in life, with practice, your ability will improve. See p. 133.

Problem solving

Being able to deal with problems can help you manage your stress. Your thinking style, as we saw on p. 64, affects how effectively you manage your life. Solving problems provides you with the chance of learning new skills.

The six-stage problem-solving model

Stage one: identify the problem

The first step is to identify exactly what is wrong. When defining a problem, it is important to be as clear and specific as possible about what exactly is troubling you (Figure 8).

You identify the problem by:

- writing down what is happening, who is involved and what you believe is wrong. For example, *situation*: dealing with heavy traffic to get the children to school on time. *Those involved*: me. *What is wrong*? I am frightened I will be late and get really stressed;
- drawing a circle in the middle of a page to represent you, and then putting all the external and internal

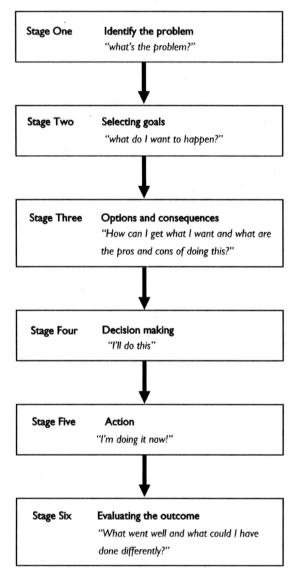

Figure 8. The six-stage problem-solving model

influences around you. For example, *an external influence* would be the actual information you need, whereas *an internal influence* might be '*feeling unsure of how to manage my stressed feelings*'.

Stage two: selecting goals

The next task is to set a goal. Your goal needs to be specific. Although '*I want to feel less stressed than I normally do*' tells you what you want, it is not specific enough. A better alternative would be '*I want to arrive at school in a calm manner regardless of whether we are late or not*'. This example states more clearly what you want to do.

If you set yourself a goal, you have to measure whether you are achieving it or not. Goals need to be specific and measurable as well as realistic. Are you one of those people who set themselves unrealistic goals? For example, '*I want to be able to do all that is asked*'. If you set yourself unrealistic goals, you are likely to be discouraged and increase your stress levels. Unless you are a mind reader, you cannot know what might happen, and no matter how hard or well you prepare it is possible that something unexpected could happen, such as a lorry shedding its load.

The next step is to make sure your goal is relevant, and the last part of the goal-setting process is to set yourself a time limit. When are you going to employ your strategies?

One way of remembering the goal-making process is to keep in mind the acronym *SMART*.

S pecific: Goals should be short and clear
e.g., '*I want to arrive at school in a calm manner.*'

M easurable: This considers how you will measure your progress.

e.g., *'I will rate my feelings on a scale of 0 – 10.'*

A chievable: Is your goal realistic?

e.g. *'If I practise my coping strategies, I am likely to handle the situation in a more productive manner than I have done.'*

R elevant: How relevant is my Goal?

e.g., *'I will feel more in control and less stressed.'*

T ime: How much time should I allocate?

e.g., *'I will use the weekend to practise my imagery exercises and then use them Monday to Friday next week when taking the children to school.'*

Stage three: options and consequences

OPTIONS

Once you have identified the problem, you need to consider the associated consequences.

BRAINSTORMING

Brainstorming is one technique you can use to help you expand your options. Brainstorming involves:

1. Writing down the issue at the top of the page.
2. Giving yourself ten minutes to come up with as many ideas as you can. As you write down your ideas you:

   - do not censor your ideas, regardless of how far-fetched you think they are;
   - go for quantity and not quality at this stage,

3. Once you have exhausted yourself in terms of your ideas, you can go back over them and see which ones seem useful and which ones you will disregard.

WHO CAN HELP YOU?

Perhaps you know someone who has dealt with a similar situation – how did they do it? If your problem is work-related, perhaps your organization offers a coaching scheme. If your problem is personal, you may have a friend or family member who can help.

CONSEQUENCES

Now that you have identified your options, you need to consider the pros and cons attached to each one. As in the cost–benefits analysis earlier, it is best to write everything down.

Brainstorming is a good tool for considering the consequences of a particular course of action. In an earlier chapter you were introduced to the power of imagery and using your imagination. You may wish to visualize your options and use your imagination to 'see' what could happen.

Stage four: decision making

Your plan may require one course of action or a series of actions. If you are unable to make a decision it may be because:

- it is impossible to solve the problem – maybe all that can be done is to manage the situation;
- you may need more information;

- you may be unclear about choosing between the various options available to you.

If you believe the problem is impossible to solve, try rewording it or breaking it down into smaller sections that are more easily resolved. If you require more information, you need to decide how to get this.

When you are confused between two or more options you may find it useful to talk to a friend or colleague. Use the rating scale (0–10) you were introduced to earlier to see if one of the options has the edge over another. Think about each option and try to visualize how you imagine things would be if you took that course of action.

HOW TO MANAGE SETBACKS

Although you have considered the pros and cons of a variety of actions, you may also find it useful to have a contingency plan worked out. A contingency plan means thinking about what to do if things do not go according to plan.

For example, if you wanted to learn to swim, what could get in the way of you doing this? How many things could go wrong, and how would you react to each of them? The 'Personal Contingency Plan' set out in Table 6? is a way of helping you think through and predict all the things that could go wrong and how you would deal with such events if they occurred. Brainstorm as many problems as you can foresee before undertaking this exercise.

You may find that some of your plans require practice; for example, practising challenging unhelpful cognitions.

Table 6.   Personal contingency plan
Feeling (rate 0–10)

What could go wrong?	What could I do if this happens?
1. 1. *Work might get in the way.* *strategies.*	1. *I need to designate a day and time and ensure that this is in my diary and that I leave on time to get to my class.*
2. *I might not always feel like going even though I want to learn to swim and it will be good for me from a health point of view.*	2. *My friend Jane wants to learn to swim too, so maybe we should go together and that way I would make sure I turned up.*
3.	3.
4.	4.
5.	5.
6.	6.

Stage five: action

Once you have made your decision you need to ensure you are fully resourced with everything you need to succeed. You may find it helpful to keep a note of every action you take, together with the associated outcome. By completing an action plan, you can tick off everything you have completed and see how each of your actions adds up to changing your situation. Some people find it helpful to place a series of reminders, or post-it notes, around the house, office, in a diary, and/or on the telephone. These post-it notes act as reminders for the things that need to be done.

145

Example
20 Jan 2010

1. Ring Jane to ask her if she would like to come to swimming classes with me and set a date to start.
2. The class is on a Tuesday evening at 7.00 p.m., so I will need to leave work by 5.30 p.m. Check my diary so I can arrange everything to be able to leave on time.

Stage six: evaluating the outcome

You are the best judge of whether your problem is solved. Using the SMART goal-setting formula mentioned earlier makes it easier to measure your success. By making your goal specific, it is easier to see how far you have gone in achieving what you set out to do. Another way is to use what is called a 'continuum', that is, a line that acts as a graded scale of how far you feel you have managed to come. Once you have drawn your line, place your X at the point that you believe most closely matches your progress.

Example

Not being able swim———X———being able to swim

If you have achieved what you set out to do, then you can bring the problem-solving process to an end. If you have made no progress at all, you need to radically overhaul the steps you have taken and the decisions you have made. You may, for example, have been rather ambitious in the goal you set yourself. It may have seemed feasible at the time, but you may have found the implementation more difficult than you anticipated. If this is the case, you need to go back to the beginning of the problem-solving process and, this time, break down the tasks into more manageable steps.

You may have identified more deep-rooted problems that you feel you cannot tackle on your own and you may require professional help. On those occasions where a partial completion of goals has been achieved, you need to consider what went well and what proved difficult. You may feel you are happy enough with what you have achieved, or you may feel that you need to take those aspects that you have been less successful with and set about a new problem-solving process with these.

Assertion training

Assertion training encourages people to use skills that build upon inner resources. Assertiveness aids clear communication with other people. Very often, people who experience stress take on too much and do not know how to say 'no' for fear of offending or seeming selfish. Assertion training provides the individual with the relevant techniques to be able to take control of his or her communications in a way that is open, but also respectful to others as well as the person concerned.

Assertiveness quiz

The following questions are designed to help you assess your behaviour patterns. Be honest in your responses and answer each question by writing the most appropriate letter in the box: Y for 'Yes', N for 'No', S for 'Sometimes', or N for 'Never'. Choose the response that most closely matches your behaviour.

1. Do you say what you feel? ☐
2. Do you make decisions easily? ☐
3. Are you critical of other people? ☐
4. Do you say something if someone pushes ☐
   in front of you?
5. Do you usually have confidence in ☐
   your own decision-making capacity? ☐
6. Do you lose your temper quickly? ☐
7. Do you find it hard to say 'No' ☐
8. Do you continue with an argument after ☐
   the other person has finished?
9. When you discover goods are faulty, ☐
   do you take them back?
10. Do you feel shy in social situations? ☐
11. Are you able to show your emotions? ☐
12. Are you able to ask people for help? ☐

Note: There is no right or wrong answer to the questions above. The answers that you have given provide you with information about your personal style of behaviour. You are now in a position to decide whether you are happy with the answers you have given and whether you would like to change the way that you behave.

Four types of behaviour

Non-assertive/passive

PERSONAL FEELINGS

A non-assertive person often feels helpless, powerless, inadequate, frustrated, and lacking in confidence.

BEHAVIOURS

Signs of being passive:

- not asking for what you want;
- not saying what you feel;
- avoiding situations where you have to make decisions;
- feeling like a victim and/or martyr;
- finding it hard to say 'no' so that you become over-committed and frustrated.

HOW OTHERS FEEL

Being around a non-assertive person can leave others feeling frustrated. You could feel sorry for the person at first, but then, having tried to help him/her and, in some cases having received no response, you end up feeling irritated and annoyed.

CONSEQUENCES

Non-assertive people avoid taking responsibility and risks. They want to avoid rejection and the decision-making process. Many people who suffer from anxiety are often passive.

EXERCISE

Circle the words that best describe you.

Helpless	Powerless	Inadequate
Frustrated	Victim	Martyr
Over-committed	Poor confidence	Avoids responsibility
Not a risk-taker	Avoids rejection	Hard on self

Aggressive

PERSONAL FEELINGS

Aggressive people often feel out of control. Although they may feel superior in the short-term, they may also feel fearful, insecure, and suffer from a lack of confidence.

SIGNS OF AGGRESSION

- you shout, bully and use verbal and/or physical force to get your own way;
- you feel you must 'win' at all costs and anything except getting your own way is 'failure';
- you do not respect the rights of other people.

HOW OTHERS FEEL

Someone exhibiting aggressive behaviour can make others feel scared, angry, helpless, and used.

CONSEQUENCES

Aggressive people tend to dominate. Their aggressive behaviour means they do not need to explain, negotiate, or listen to others. However, in the longer term, an aggressive person may become isolated and lose the respect of others.

EXERCISE

Circle the words that best describe you.

Shouts   Hits objects   Bullies others   Wags finger

Superior Fearful   Insecure   Poor confidence

Indirectly aggressive/passive–aggressive

PERSONAL FEELINGS

When you behave in a passive–aggressive manner you may feel frustrated, disappointed, and lacking in confidence.

SIGNS OF INDIRECTLY AGGRESSIVE/ PASSIVE–AGGRESSIVE BEHAVIOURS

- You are unpredictable. One day you agree and the next you disagree about the same subject.
- You hold grudges and bide your time to pay back others.
- You sulk and are able to generate a difficult atmosphere around you.

HOW OTHERS FEEL

When you are around a passive–aggressive person, you may find yourself feeling angry, hurt, confused, manipulated, and guilty.

CONSEQUENCES

This type of behaviour is aimed at avoiding direct confrontation and rejection and often leads to a breakdown in relationships.

EXERCISE

Circle the words that best describe you.

Frustrated   Disappointed   Lacking in confidence

Holds grudges Uses 'pay-back' Sulks

Avoids confrontation

Assertive

PERSONAL FEELINGS

An assertive person often feels relaxed and confident. Assertiveness does not provide immunity against experiencing difficult emotions and an assertive person has a full range of emotions. However, an assertive person can choose the appropriate behaviour to use.

SIGNS OF ASSERTIVENESS

- I ask for what I want;
- I attempt to be clear in what I say;
- I listen to the needs of others;
- I respect myself and other people;
- I aim for 'win–win' situations and am happy to compromise without seeing compromising as something negative.

HOW OTHERS REACT

If you are around an assertive person, you will usually feel valued, respected, and listened to. An assertive person's behaviour makes people feel safe, secure, and fairly treated.

CONSEQUENCES

Assertive people seize opportunities, develop healthy relationships, and feel genuinely confident.

Exercise

Circle the words that best describe you.

Confident   Relaxed   Listens to others

Win–win   Seizes opportunities Respects others

Respects self

Assertiveness involves respect for self and for others

Assertive people respect themselves and other people equally. They choose to show this respect in the way they openly, honestly, and genuinely deal with other people. They will stand up for themselves. Setting boundaries is one way in which we show respect for ourselves. It is up to each individual to decide what boundaries to create.

For example, '*I appreciate that you are unable to provide me with that information. However, I would appreciate it if you could pass me on to someone who can*'.

Taking personal responsibility for thoughts, feelings, and actions

Assertive people are prepared to take responsibility for what they say, for what they feel, and for what they do. They realize how important it is to act in a responsible way.

For example, '*I feel you are not listening to me when you look at your Blackberry while we are talking*' is more assertive than '*You never listen to me and are so rude.*' Using the word 'I' is one way of taking responsibility for what you feel, think, say, and do, for example, '*I feel unhappy about what you have just said*'.

Recognizing and making choices

Assertive people recognize the need to make choices and do not avoid doing so. They believe that even if they make the wrong choice, it is not the end of the world. Assertiveness means taking risks and assertive people believe that life is based on acceptable risk-taking.

Some assertiveness skills

The three steps to assertiveness

STEP ONE

Listen to what the other person is saying and demonstrate that you have *heard* and *understood* what has been said. You are more likely to get the outcome you seek if the other person feels you have really heard him/her. Very often we are more concerned with what we want to say than what the other person has said, and this can lead to the pantomime situation of '*oh yes you did, oh no, I didn't*'.

Andrew: '*I felt a bit annoyed when you bought a sofa for the living room without consulting me.*'
Mary: '*I can see how you might have felt that.*'

STEP TWO

In step two you say what you *think* or *feel*. If this stage is to flow smoothly, you need to use a *link* word or phrase such as 'however', or 'on the other hand', or 'alternatively'.

Mary: '*However, it was on special offer and so much
             cheaper and I knew we would lose it and I could
             not get hold of you.*'

STEP THREE

In step three you say what you *want to happen*. To help
this section flow from the one before you need to use the
link word *and*. In step three you are looking for what
could be called a workable compromise, something that
will sort the situation out and help both parties learn
something useful for the next time such a situation arises.

Andrew: '*I can see that would cause you a dilemma. I
            would prefer to be in on the decision-making
            wherever possible.*

Example

Step one: 'I appreciate that it's important for us to see
             your mum . . .'
Link word: . . . *however,*
Step two: '*Seeing her every Sunday does not allow us to
             do anything else on that day*'
Link word: *and*
Step three: '*I would like it if we could find alternative
             days and ways to make sure we get to see your
             mum, but without limiting all our Sundays.*'

Managing instant reactions

Change takes time. If you find yourself reacting quickly,
count to three in your head and take a deep breath. This

should slow you down so that you can make a more considered response.

Less is more

You may find you over-explain yourself in the answers you give. If this is the case, try to keep what you say short and simple. After all, you can have more than one bite of the apple and do not have to say everything in one go.

More assertiveness skills

Broken record

There will be times when you have used the three-step model and the person seems to ignore what you say. In this case, you need to repeat what you have said in a consistent way until your message cannot be ignored. The idea is to restate the essence of what you are saying rather than always using the same words

Example

Gayle: '*I appreciate you want agree the office plans today.*'
James: '*Surely you can give me some idea now?*'
Gayle: '*I can understand that it is frustrating for you. However, the plans are in constant change and I would have to go through it all again at the end of the month when they are finalized.*'

Negative feelings assertion

You need to identify the behaviour that troubles you, explain how it affects you, and say what you want to happen. For example, if someone is shouting at you, you may find it hard to listen to what is being said and you can say so. If the person is sulking, you may feel that you cannot get through to him/her to sort out what is wrong and this damages your feelings towards that person.

Example

'*I feel disappointed when you don't listen to what I have to say and keep looking at your Blackberry* (the behaviour) *and find that I don't want to carry on the conversation* (how it affects you) *and I do want us to discuss things fully and have your full attention*' (what you want to happen).

Workable compromise

This works on the basis of finding a solution that both of you can live with. It is about aiming for a 'win–win' situation, and it means both of you compromising to find a solution that you are happy with. People who aim to communicate in this way increase their bank of goodwill, as they see goodwill as a kind of investment that can be called upon later.

Example

Karin: '*I really need you to help me with my computer.*'
Damian: '*I'm really happy to help you. However, I am a bit busy at the moment and will come over at about 7.00 p.m. tonight to do it.*'
Karin: '*Thanks, I would appreciate that.*'

Deflecting

Deflecting can be used to diffuse aggressive situations. It is based on the principle that no one is perfect and requires

157

you only to agree that the person making the statement has a right to his or her own point of view. If you agree with the person you are not selling out, simply acknowledging their right to their own view. Most people are waiting for us to disagree with them and all this disagreement gains is a game of *'oh yes you did – oh no I didn't.'* If you agree with part of what is being said, you can stop the situation from escalating.

Example

Maud: 'You always talk over me.' (This sort of statement could easily lead to a row.)

Suzie: *'I don't mean to, but I do sometimes get carried away, so perhaps I do without realizing it.'* (By agreeing only to the possibility, you act in a way that defuses a potentially explosive situation.)

Discrepancy assertion

This skill simply requires you to highlight any inconsistencies in what is being said.

Example

'On the one hand you say you say I never have enough time for you, and on the other you say that you find I'm always making too many suggestions.'

Thinking it over time

Changing behaviour takes time. If you have been someone who says 'yes' without thinking, you may find yourself continuing to do so. One way of breaking the cycle is to ask for 'thinking it over time'. When asked something, take time to consider your position. If you are on the telephone, suggest that you ring the person back at a certain time – '*I can't speak now so let me ring you back in twenty minutes*'. If you are actually with someone, you can say, '*I need time to think about what you have said*'.

A quick trip to the loo is an effective way to buy time. A quick '*excuse me*' followed by a few minutes taking time to think about what you want to say can provide the space you need to make a sensible decision.

My personal rights

EXERCISE

Consider the following statements and mark each box with 'A' or 'D' depending on whether you agree or disagree with them.

- I have the right to be treated with respect as an equal human being. ☐
- I have the right to ask for what I want ☐
- I have the right to look after my needs and say 'No'. ☐
- I have the right to express my feelings and thoughts ☐
- I have the right to ask for time before making a decision ☐
- I have the right to make my own decisions ☐
- I have the right to change my mind ☐
- I have the right to refuse responsibility for other people's problems if I so choose ☐
- I have the right to choose not to be assertive ☐

These rights are a way to get you thinking about how you value yourself. Alongside rights are also the responsibilities we have towards others. Assertiveness means respecting self and others equally. You do not have the right to infringe the rights of others and you give yourself the same rights you give other people.

EXERCISE

What other rights do you want to add to those above?

Dealing with difficult situations

Coping with conflict

No one gets through life without having to face conflict. Most people dislike conflict but many of us make the situation worse by the way we deal with it. Stressed people often avoid conflict and then feel put upon or not valued.

Assertiveness skills provide you with a set of skills to deal with what is said so that you can verbally influence a positive outcome.

Work towards a win–win outcome

Try to think about what you want and what you think the other person might want. See if you can give the other person something of what they want as this is more likely to make them amenable and get you more of what you want with the least hassle.

Separate yourself and the other person from the issue

When the temperature rises and when you want something, emotions such as anxiety can get in the way. Strong emotions block the ability to listen and think – both of which are required if conflict is to be resolved without damaging the relationship. When we are stressed we can often find that even small situations can trigger strong emotions.

Take responsibility and make clear 'I' statements

You are responsible for your own thoughts and actions. If you want to handle conflict assertively, you need to ensure you make clear 'I' statements as a way of demonstrating your needs and wants.

One issue at a time, and know what you want to happen

Your conflict with a person may be about one issue or about many issues. You might find you have bottled things up and that there is a danger of too many subjects being talked about at the same time. Successful conflict resolution means dealing with one subject at a time. This means making a list of all the things you want to talk about and then deciding which one to discuss first.

Give your undivided attention

You are far more likely to get a positive outcome if you can demonstrate your respect for the other person by the way you deal with them.

The right time and the right place

If you really want to resolve a situation, then think about when and where you are going to deal with it. There is also little point in trying to resolve conflict if you are likely to be disturbed or in a crowded place. Choose a private location and a time when both of you are free.

Dealing with requests

There are times when people will ask you to do something for them. If you are happy to say yes to a request, then fine. However, many people say yes when they really want to say no. There are four steps for dealing with requests.

STEP ONE: WHAT YOU FEEL

Many people override their basic 'gut' reaction to a request and some people not only override it, they also don't notice it. When someone makes a request, you may find yourself feeling uncomfortable in some way. If this is the case, ask yourself what you feel uncomfortable about. It may also help you to ask yourself the following questions.

- *Do I feel used in some way?*
- *Do I feel 'I have to' and, if so, why?*
- *What's the worst that could happen if I say no?*
- *What feeling am I experiencing* (stress, anger, fear, embarrassment, etc.)?

STEP TWO: SAYING 'NO'

If you want to say 'no', say so clearly. It is perfectly reasonable to provide an explanation, but do not excuse or justify yourself. If you over-explain it usually means you feel bad about saying no and are trying to justify your position.

STEP THREE: SAYING 'YES'

If you want to say 'yes', say so clearly. If you are happy to say yes but want to modify what you are prepared to offer, then outline the conditions that apply

STEP FOUR: NOT SURE

If you are not sure what you want:

- ask for more information to help you make your decision;
- ask for more time to consider your decision;
- suggest a compromise if you believe this is appropriate;
- watch out for an 'indirect no' – a way of trying to avoid saying no by stating things in ways that are aimed at getting the other person to take back the request.

Handling criticism

Many people believe that criticism means that they are inadequate in some way or are being unfairly targeted, as mentioned earlier.

You can handle criticism by:

- being clear about what the criticism is about. Ask for more information;

163

- asking for more time to consider what has been said. After all, it can be difficult to identify what you think or feel immediately;
- asking for more information, if required, and then stating clearly your need for time to consider what has been said. Wherever possible, tell the person when you will come back to him/her;
- once you have thought about what has been said, you need to decide whether you think the criticism is valid or not. If you agree with what has been said, you need to accept the criticism and discuss any future changes. If you disagree with what has been said, then ensure you disagree confidently, making sure you do not apologize.

Giving criticism

Giving criticism can be as hard for some people as receiving it, especially for people who suffer from stress. It can seem like asking for trouble, since the stressed person usually just wants to keep his or her head down. Holding on to negative feelings doesn't help. If you are a manager, you will have to give criticism to your staff at some time or another. If you are a parent, you will have to criticize your children from time to time, otherwise they may never learn and could go on to develop unhelpful ways of relating to others.

You can give criticism effectively by:

- finding a private place to have the discussion. If you want someone to think about what you are saying you need to respect his or her feelings;

- finding something good to say about the person's behaviour. Acknowledge the person's good points as well as bad points. Be genuine in what you say;
- trying to avoid becoming too personal. Keep your comments to the facts of the situation and how you feel;
- criticizing the person's behaviour. Behaviour is something you have control over, whereas there may be things about the person that they cannot change: for example, that they speak with an accent;
- describing your feelings and how you are affected by the person's behaviour;
- making sure you listen to what the other person has to say. Effective communication requires active participation and active listening;
- ensuring that the other person needs to understand the consequence of not changing. If someone knows that a particular behaviour upsets you or damages your relationship, this can be enough to motivate him or her to change.

Managing put-downs

There are a number of different ways in which people may try to put you down, some of which are listed below.

1. *Making decisions for you*
   Trying to make a decision for you puts you down as it takes away your personal responsibility. If this is the case, you need to let the person know you are capable of making your own decisions. For example, '*I appreciate you have my best interests at heart. However, I need to do this myself.*'

165

2. *Putting the pressure on you*

   Sometimes people drop something on us when we are least expecting it as a way of trying to force us to make a decision or go along with what they are saying. This type of action puts you on the spot. If this is the case, you need to ask for time to think about what is being asked of you.

3. *Making claims that you are lying*

   A person may suggest directly or indirectly that what you have said is not true, the implication being that you are lying. If this is the case, you need to be clear about what you are saying. For example, '*It is my understanding that Jane was the last person to leave the office.*'

Using the 'traffic light' system

We have explored the concept of you recognizing your 'early warning systems' when it comes to experiencing stress – for example, learning that when you find yourself breathing faster, or fidgeting, or feeling hot. these physical reactions tell you that you are becoming stressed and emotional. In addition, we have also considered the way that you judge situations and the types of 'faulty thinking' you may engage in, and we have also considered the reality that change takes time.

One technique that some people have found helpful is that of using the imagery of a traffic light to help manage difficult situations.

Red   =   Stop
Amber =   Wait
Green =   Go

Red

When you are in a situation and feel your stress rising because this situation is either one of your triggers or because you recognize that you are getting emotional, you visualize the red stop sign.

Amber

Now that you have stopped, you wait, and during this period you undertake whatever strategies you need so that you gain the ability to control what you say and what you will do. For example, you may undertake the rescue remedy breathing exercise, or you identify your faulty thinking, or you think about using the three-step model from the assertiveness section of this book. This is the stage where you wait, analyse, and plan what to do.

Green

Now that you have stopped (red), waited and planned (amber), you can now take whatever action seems appropriate as you have the Green light to go! By the time you get to Green you are more likely to act in a way that is helpful to you and to others.

The role of 'time out'

Although you may be very committed to changing your behaviour, you may not find it easy to overcome the unhelpful habits that you have fallen into. Sometimes it is best to walk away from a situation to give yourself time to calm down. If you get upset with your partner when certain types of discussions come up, then it might be helpful if you agree with him or her that if you recognize that you are likely to get out of control you will engage in a strategy called 'time out'. Time out means walking away to another room, to engage in another activity until you can think clearly, or even going for a walk to cool down.

Time out is a short-term strategy, and one which is really useful as a fall-back position for those situations where it all gets out of hand and you fear you may act in a self-defeating manner and/or become overwhelmed.

The more you practise the other techniques in this book, the less you will need to use time out.

Learning how to argue

While some people avoid arguing by becoming ultra passive and refusing to say what they feel, others think that arguments provide an opportunity to insult the other person – often believing the only way to argue is to make sure you scream the loudest. There are also those that fall into a massive sulk the minute you disagree with whatever they say or do. All these behaviours harm a relationship – they make you feel bad about yourself and usually end up with both of you feeling hurt and rejected and you never really sort out the cause of the original disagreement.

Arguments are a part of life. You are not going to get to your deathbed without having an argument with someone, somewhere, at some time. The good news is – there is such a thing as a healthy argument. Healthy arguing takes practice and can be learned like any skill, and once you have cracked how to do it you'll find your disagreements far more productive.

If you want to strengthen your relationship, you need to learn how to disagree. Healthy arguing means you get to know each other better – after all, how can you know what someone is like if you never find out what they think? Learning how to argue will help you to communicate more clearly and you will end up feeling more respect for yourself and for others.

If you want to argue more successfully with family, friends, partners, your boss, and your work colleagues, then the following tips will help you.

Listen!

Start by listening to what the other person has to say and make sure you acknowledge their point of view. You do not have to agree with what they are saying, but you do need to show you've got the message. For example, '*I can see that you might feel I'm not always thoughtful*', or '*I get the feeling you sometimes feel I don't listen to you*'. If you don't actively show that you have listened, the other person will assume you haven't and will either walk away or withdraw because they will think you're not taking them seriously. Alternatively, they may increase the intensity of their argument and the volume of their voice in an attempt to make you listen.

Think about what is being said

It's all right to ask for time to think about what is being said. You don't have to answer instantly, and you can come back to the discussion later. Make sure you tell the other person you need time to think, otherwise you could end up looking as if you're the one avoiding the issue rather than simply needing some space and time to think about it! Make the point that you respect what they have to say, and, therefore, you believe they deserve a proper answer.

So you're always right then?

Does the other person have a point? If you think they do, agree, if not, state your reasons for disagreeing in as calm a way as possible. You may need more information before you can decide whether they do have a point or not, and if this is the case don't be afraid to ask for it. After all, how you can you decide one way or the other if you don't know what the other person is really talking about?

Stick to the point

Don't get side-tracked into other issues. Take one thing at a time. Make a list if you have to, but keep to the point. Think about what you are trying to get out of the argument – for example, if you want to make a point, do so clearly and keep on repeating it as long as it takes to get the point home. Remember that this is not about getting the other person to agree with you (although that would be nice), but simply about them hearing your point of view.

Don't try and talk about too many things at once. Very often when an argument starts it is tempting to bring up all sorts of events that you feel the other person did not handle well. However, all this does is to prolong the argument and ends up like scoring points . . . 'and another thing . . .!'

Don't put off discussions for too long

If you put off having a discussion for too long it may mean that both of you have time for your feelings to fester. When you do this, what usually happens is you end up arguing about something else that is totally unrelated! Don't put your head in the sand. So many arguments could be avoided if people shared all the little things that bug them when they happen. People often tell me they don't want to say anything because it might sound petty. However, it's all those petty things that get stored up that one day are let out all at once, usually in a major argument over nothing at all.

Don't blame others

You are responsible for your *own feelings* – it is too easy to blame others. People are *not mind readers* – just because you think something doesn't mean the other person has to, or that you are right. People are brought up differently, with different rules about how to behave and, if you assume that all people should think the way you do, it will only lead to problems.

Can you remember the first time you went to a friend's house and saw his or her family doing something differently to your own? – I imagine you thought it was odd, and up until that point you had thought everyone did everything the way your family did.

Back to that 'win–win'

Many people approach arguments as if they are a life and death situation. Research has shown that successful and happy people look for a 'win–win' in their disagreements with others. Compromise is not a dirty word – those who know how to compromise usually end up far better off than those who don't. What is the point of hurting your relationship just to prove you were right?

Yes, and back to listening, too

The ability to handle difficult situations and hold a conversation depends on being able to develop active listening skills. Good listening skills help you get to know the person you are speaking to and are also crucial in deepening relationships and helping sort out problems.

You need to *learn* how to:

LISTEN: to what the other person is saying and feed back the essence of what they are saying. Hold on to what you have to say until the other person has completed what he or she has to say.

EVALUATE/EMPATHISE: remember what has been said and see if you can make connections. For example: *'You said earlier that you thought I had not been listening and I can imagine this must have been irritating'*. Does it sound as if the person is happy, sad, enthusiastic, or indifferent? Try to use these feelings in your conversation. For example: *'You sound quite cross'*. Empathy is the ability to be to put yourself in the other person's shoes. When someone talks to you, try to imagine how you would feel if you saw the world the way that person does.

And

RESPOND: a good listener is involved in the conversation and can sometimes anticipate what the speaker is going to say next. Don't complete people's sentences, but try to imagine where you think the conversation is going. Don't be frightened to add information of your own. For example: *'I know what you mean about how I can come across as distracted, I find that hard when other people do that to me'*. To learn to become proficient at active listening takes time and practice. Active listening means developing your memory and concentration skills, and these do get better in time. Try using these skills in as many places and with as many people as possible.

Now: although it is helpful to plan for difficult conversations, it is also important to deal with situations as soon as you can. If you put things off then feelings can fester.

THE STRESS-FREE DIET

Stress and dietary tips

Stress can be made worse by taking stimulants such as tea, coffee, colas, and chocolate, all of which contain caffeine. Caffeine is a stimulant, and stimulants are best avoided when we are experiencing stress. Because we produce stress hormones when we are feeling stressed, this can affect our blood sugar levels and they may indeed drop dramatically. Therefore, in order to keep those levels balanced, it is important to eat 'little and often' during the day. It may also be helpful to avoid refined sugars and other substances which 'give too much of a high' too quickly. Slow-release foods such as carbohydrates (potatoes, pasta, rice, bread, apples, and bananas) are a much better idea, as they fuel the body in a more even, controlled way.

These days it is impossible to avoid information on healthy eating. However, what we eat also has an effect on our confidence levels and our ability to cope emotionally.

As was outlined in the 'Stress busting' section earlier in this book, our bodies produce stress hormones and release fatty acids and sugars to help us cope with a perceived crisis. When such events take place our bodies natural blood sugar levels are disturbed. Our blood sugars help us to regulate the fuel requirements needed by our bodies. Low blood sugar or hypoglycaemia contributes to symptoms of stress.

A drop in blood sugar causes reactions in the nervous system, including feelings of anxiety or irritability. Diets that contain large amounts of refined sugars, or are deficient in protein or fat, together with the use of stimulants such as coffee or cola based drinks, contribute to this condition.

You may be lacking in magnesium, zinc, and the amino acid tryptophan. Alternatively, an excessive amount of some nutrients can speed up your nervous system and this can provide the breeding ground for stress. Potassium, sodium, phosphorus, and copper are just such minerals.

If the thyroid or adrenal glands become overactive, such conditions affect the way we feel, as we cannot absorb and use sufficient minerals and, as a result, difficult to manage emotions may follow. An underactive thyroid is more likely to lead to feelings of depression than of anxiety.

What can I do to help myself?

If you have any concerns at all about your health, your first port of call should always be your doctor. I have always believed that all medical conditions should be eliminated before considering any emotional and/or life factors.

We are all aware that eating a healthy diet is good for our overall health. However, there is research that suggests that eating certain types of food can have a positive effect on the way in which we behave. For example, you will see that under 'What foods can I eat?' I have listed fish/shellfish under protein. The reason for this is that omega-3 DHA (an essential fatty acid) has been linked with helping control behavioural conditions such as depression, alcoholism, and aggressive behaviour.

The following are some dietary tips that will help you.

- Drink plenty of water – not only is it good for your skin, it helps to flush out toxins and keeps your kidneys in good working order. Around eight large glasses a day is best. There is nothing wrong with flavouring the water if you are not keen on drinking water. However, avoid sugary flavourings as this will defeat the object. Drinking fruit teas are also a good way of getting water into you.
- Make sure you eat at least six times a day. Breakfast, mid-morning, lunch, mid-afternoon, tea, and dinner. By eating little and often and ensuring that you do not skip meals you will help your blood sugar levels stay balanced.
- Keep healthy snacks around you and plan ahead for days when it may be difficult to find healthy meals.
- Try to avoid 'fast food', as it usually contains more fat and additives than are good for you.
- Take a multi-vitamin pill daily. It can be difficult to ensure you get all the nutrients you need through the food you eat and a multi-vitamin tablet will help to ensure you are topped up on any you may be missing. A good option for people who don't like fish is to take omega-3 DHA capsules. However, it is best if you can get your vitamins directly from the food you eat, rather than from vitamin pills.
- Try to avoid coffee, tea, cola drinks, and chocolate, as all these contain varying amounts of caffeine. It would be a sad world if you could not allow yourself a little of what you fancy, so if you want chocolate now and again, buy the more expensive kind which has a higher concentration of cocoa solids and less sugar.

- Try to avoid saturated fats, as these can lead to health problems. A diet that is high in fat will also contain high levels of cholesterol. There is an increased risk of cancer of the breast, colon, and prostate, as well as coronary heart disease.
- Try to avoid an excess of alcohol – alcohol dehydrates, is a depressant, and can increase depressive symptoms, mood swings, and fuel aggression. In addition, alcohol, rather than aiding sleep, actually impairs it, and when you are tired you are likely to be more irritable. In addition, it can deplete vitamin B levels in the body and vitamin B is linked with aiding a healthy nervous system.
- Avoid excessive amounts of salt (sodium), as about a quarter of what we require is to be found naturally present in food. We require so little that we can quite happily survive on what occurs in our daily food.

What food can I eat?

The aim is to eat as varied a diet as possible. However, the following categories provide you with a more detailed breakdown of a range of foods which contribute to good physical and psychological health.

Protein

- Meat, chicken.
- Fish, shellfish (omega-3 DHA is an essential fatty acid and the best source is oily fish such as salmon, mackerel, sardines, and tuna).
- Dried beans.
- Soya products.

Carbohydrates

COMPLEX

- Wholegrain bread.
- Pasta.
- Rice.
- Peas and beans.
- Vegetables.
- Fruit and nuts.

Refined sugar (not so helpful)

- Sweet foods.

Calcium

- Milk, cheese, yoghurt.
- Fish.
- Broccoli, spring greens, leeks, cabbage, parsnips, potatoes, blackberries, and oranges.

Potassium

- Potatoes and sweet potatoes.
- Fish, sardines.
- Pork, chicken.
- Cauliflower, sweetcorn, avocados, leeks.
- Breakfast cereals.
- Natural yoghurt.
- Bananas, rhubarb.

Iron

- Eggs.
- Lean meat.
- Wholegrain cereals.

- Peas, beans, spinach, leeks, broccoli, spring greens, potatoes, avocados.
- Dried fruit

Zinc and copper

- Liver and kidney, chicken
- Oysters.
- Soya flour, cocoa powder.
- Rice, bulgar wheat.
- Beans, parsnips, plantain.
- Pears.

WHAT TYPE OF HELP
IS AVAILABLE?

The Royal College of Psychiatrists and the International Stress Management Association has recommended a number of ways in which an individual can seek help.

Talking about the problem

This can help when the stress comes from recent knocks, like a spouse leaving, a child becoming ill, bereavement, or losing a job. Who should we talk to? Try friends or relatives whom you trust, whose opinions you respect, and who are good listeners. They may have had the same problem themselves, or know someone else who has. As well as having the chance to talk, you may be able to find out how other people have coped with a similar problem.

Learning to relax

It can be very beneficial to learn a special way of relaxing to help to control stress and tension. Such techniques can be learnt through groups or through professionals, but there are also self-help books and videotapes (see below). It is a good idea to practise these regularly, not just when we are in a crisis situation.

Psychological therapies

This is a more intensive talking treatment that can help people to understand and to come to terms with the reasons for their stress that they may not have recognized themselves. The treatment can take place in groups or individually, and is usually weekly for several weeks or months. Therapists may or may not be medically qualified.

There are specialist stress counsellors, coaches, and stress management practitioners and, if talking to your family or friends does not work, such a specialist could be of assistance. Make sure that the person has undertaken a cognitive–behavioural training of some sort, as much of the research has indicated that much of what we call stress relates back to the way we think.

USEFUL RESOURCES

Association for Coaching
66 Church Road
London
W7 1LB
www.associationforcoaching.com

Association for Rational Emotive Behaviour Therapy
2nd Floor
2 Walsworth Road
Hitchin
Hertfordshire
SG4 9SP.
www.arebt.org
A professional body that can provide details of therapists.

British Association for Counselling and Psychotherapy
15 St John's Business Park
Lutterworth
LE17 4HB,
Tel: 01455 883300,
www.counselling.co.uk
A professional body that can provide lists of therapists as
well as information and advice on counselling.

British Association for Behavioural and Cognitive
Psychotherapies
Victoria Buildings
9–13 Silver Street
Bury
BL9 0EU
Tel: 0161 797 4484
www.babcp.com

A professional body that can provide lists of therapists and also information on cognitive–behavioural psychotherapies.

British Psychological Society
St Andrew's House
48 Princess Road East
Leicester
LE1 7DR.
Tel: 0116 254 9568
www.bps.org.uk
A professional body for that can provide details of psychologists.

COSCA (Confederation of Scottish Counselling Agencies)
16 Melville Terrace
Stirling
FK8 2NE
Tel: 01786 475 140
www.cosca.org.uk
A professional body in Scotland that can provide details of counsellors and information on counselling and counselling services.

CRUSE Bereavement Care
Cruse House
126 Sheen Road
Richmond
Surrey TW9 1UR
Tel: 0208 940 4818
www.crusebereavementcare.org.uk
Offers information, advice, and counselling to those who have been bereaved, with local branch offices across the country.

International Stress Management Association (UK)
PO BOX 491
Bradley
Stoke,
Bristol
BS34 9AH,
Tel: 01179 697284
www.isma.org.uk
A professional body that provides information, advice, and
details of stress management practitioners and trainers.

Samaritans
10 The Grove
Slough
Berkshire
Tel: 01753 532713 or 0345 90 90 90
www.befrienders.org
Offers telephone counselling and drop-in centres

UKCP (United Kingdom Council for Psychotherapy)
2nd Floor
Edward House
2 Wakley Street
London EC1V 7LT
Tel: 020 7014 9955
www.psychotherapy.org.uk
A professional body with a register of psychotherapists in
the UK.

APPENDICES

Situation	Self defeating thinking	Feelings and actions	Healthy response	New approach
A	B	C	D	E

Faulty thinking form

Mood form		
Situation	Good mood	Bad mood
I think . . .	I think . . .	

Understanding what upsets me

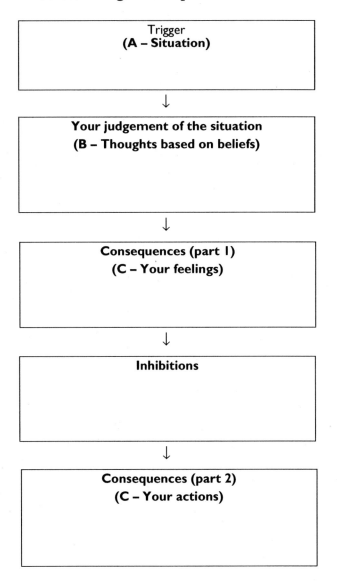

Trigger
(A – Situation)

↓

**Your judgement of the situation
(B – Thoughts based on beliefs)**

↓

**Consequences (part 1)
(C – Your feelings)**

↓

Inhibitions

↓

**Consequences (part 2)
(C – Your actions)**

Stress diary

Date	Time	Situation (trigger)	What I did

Cost–benefit analysis

Name:	Date:
Situation:	

COST	BENEFIT

Personal contingency plan

Feeling (rate 0–10)	
What could go wrong?	What could I do if this happens?
1.	1.
2.	2.
3.	3.
4.	4.
5.	5.
6.	6.

Big I, little I

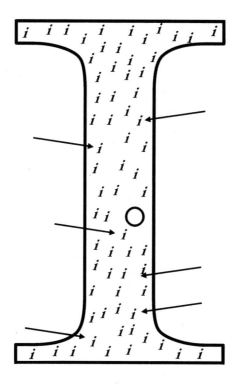

A–E Model	
A–E	Taking Stock
Adversity	
Beliefs	
Consequences	
Dispute	
Energy	

CONTACT ME

I am keen to know if my books are of help to readers and in what ways I can improve the information provided. If you would like to comment, you can email me at info@gladeanamcmahon.com, or you can send a letter to me via the publishers of this book.

INDEX

195